THE FAMILY TRAVELER'S HANDBOOK

Inspiring families to see the world together

The Family Traveler's Handbook: Inspiring families to see the world together

Library and Archives Canada Cataloguing in Publication

Gorman, Mara, 1970-, author
        The family traveler's handbook : inspiring families to
see the world together / Mara Gorman.

ISBN 978-1-927557-05-1

        1. Travel. 2. Children--Travel. 3. Family recreation.
I. Title.

G151.G67 2013   910.2   C2013-905175-9
                                              C2013-905176-7

Disclaimer:

This book provides entertaining and informative snapshots of the author's personal experiences while traveling with her family, as well as anecdotes from other travelers. As such, the Family Traveler's Handbook is not meant to serve as an exclusive checklist to effectively safeguard the reader in every family travel situation, and is sold with the understanding that neither the author nor the publisher intend to render any type of medical, psychological, or professional advice. No one can guarantee safety and travel can expose everyone to potential risks. Because safety is impacted by each person's actions and choices, each reader assumes all responsibilities and obligations with respect to any decisions or advice made or given as a result of the use of any content in this book. While all reasonable measures have been taken to ensure the quality, reliability, and accuracy of the information in the Family Traveler's Handbook, author and publisher make no warranties or guarantees, expressed or implied, by including any content herein. Neither the author or publisher, nor any contributor, will be liable for damages arising out of or in connection with the use of this book. Because of the dynamic nature of online media, certain web addresses or links contained in this book may have changed since publication and may no longer be valid.

For Tommy and Teddy

Acknowledgements

I'd like to start by thanking Janice Waugh, who, although she had not yet met me in person, not only had the faith to ask me to write this book but offered help at every stage of its development.

So many blogger and writer friends generously shared their stories, expertise, feedback, and moral support. Thank you to Kara Williams, Matt Villano, Jennifer Leo, Heather Greenwood Davis, Christine Koh, Corinne McDermott, Jodi Ettenberg, Keryn Means, Anne Taylor Hartzell, Nicole Wiltrout, Michael Lanza, Nicole Wears, Carol Cain, Debi Huang, Ashley Steel, Jessica Bowers, Amy Whitley, Rainer Jenss, Sandra Foyt, Mary Turner, Meg Nesterov, Dana Freeman, Holly Rosen Fink, Nicole Feliciano, and Peter West Carey.

I'm so grateful to my friends, parents themselves, who took time from their busy schedule to read a draft of the book. Amy Shay offered thoughtful, intelligent, and specific feedback that greatly improved my original draft. Rachel Alembakis not only cheered me on, she gave the manuscript a valuable seal of approval from a long-haul flight veteran.

Thanks also to Nina and Frank Warren for providing the lovely and quiet haven of their beach house to write my first draft.

Last, but far from least, this project would never have happened without the unfailing support, encouragement, patience, and humor of my husband, Matt Kinservik. He gave me time and space to write, read the manuscript, and offered exacting and funny feedback. I can't think of anyone who would make a better companion in travel and in life. Thank you.

Table of Contents

Table of Contents

The Backstory: How I Became a Traveling Parent

I'll never forget the first trip my husband Matt and I took with our first son, Tommy, when he was just four days old. It must have taken me half an hour just to check and re-check the diaper bag, to make sure I had all the supplies I needed. Then I had to make sure Tommy was strapped securely into his infant seat. By the time I got him in, he was crying and clearly needed to be nursed, so out he came for another half hour. Then, his diaper was wet – in fact, so were his clothes. We got him changed and settled and then – finally –we were out the door.

How enormous the world seemed, and how small and vulnerable I felt there on the sidewalk in front of my house. And all of this work was required just to put my baby in his stroller and walk down our block to visit some neighbors. By the time we got home, I felt as though I had climbed Mount Everest. How was it possible that I would ever leave my street again, let alone take a longer or more ambitious trip?

I'm not sure precisely when my perspective shifted and I felt prepared to contemplate family travel, but I do know that Tommy played a role in that shift. From the moment he could hold his head up, he was always looking around and ahead.

One day, as I walked down the street with him strapped to my chest, facing outward as usual, a 20-something, carefree young man touched my arm as I walked past. "Wow! I just have to tell you that your son is so alert!" he said. "I've never seen a baby that looked around so much and seemed so excited by the world." Fearless and engaged, that was my boy. It made me feel the same way, despite the fog of new motherhood and the equally new feeling of uncertainty that it brought.

Of course, I wanted to go places too, an impulse bred in me from a young age. When I was eight, my parents divorced; my mother responded to the trauma by taking my sister and me to Italy for nine months shortly afterward. She wasn't much of a planner and our travel narrative was one of closed currency-exchange centers, nearly missed connections, and rides in third-class train cars on wooden benches.

I have an especially vivid memory of running down a crowded train platform as she frantically searched for our car. Just as she hopped on board the train, the bungee cord flew off the small metal luggage rack that I was pulling, and sleeping bags and luggage tumbled to the ground. Breathless and frantic, I started tossing the items to her, hauling myself up the steps just as the train started to move.

But I also remember chasing pigeons in Florence by the pink and green confection of the Duomo, tasting roasted chicken skin flavored with rosemary and olive oil, peering at the silky water of the Arno from the Ponte San Trinita, and staring through the branches of an olive tree at a deep springtime sky. Even as a child, I understood the pleasure of discovering the beauty of an unfamiliar place.

I spent my junior year of college in Paris, and since then have collected other travel experiences like lovely beads on a necklace: Venice, Bath, Santorini, Mumbai, and a long roster of cities in North America. There is virtually no place that does not appeal to me. I am one of those people who read the travel section of the Sunday paper avidly, with a sense of genuine opportunity.

It's probably no surprise that it didn't take Matt and me long to decide to legitimately hit the road with Tommy. Around the time he was three months old, we cooked up a simple plan in our sleep-deprived bliss: we would drive from our home in Delaware to Kansas City to visit my best friend. But we couldn't drive all the way out there without stopping to see Matt's family in Wisconsin on the way back. And if we stopped to see them, then we had to make sure we passed through Vermont where my father and stepmother lived. And before you could say 'family travel' we were on a three-week, 4,000-mile trek through 15 American states and one Canadian province.

Now, some people might have waited until their child was a little older, until he was sleeping through the night or nursing less often. But we were so captivated by Tommy, so thrilled with our new status as parents, so eager for Tommy to be held by many loving arms, that we simply could not wait. Instead, we chose to drive for 60 hours and stay in a string of chain hotels, in places ranging from Bettendorf to Buffalo, so we could visit our large, extended family.

As this all played out, I realized how different it was to travel with an infant. No, I couldn't pump breast milk in the car even if Matt was in the driver's seat. Yes, I could amuse Tommy with finger puppets for an hour at a stretch. My education was immediate and visceral. I nursed my child in gas-station bathrooms and in mossy hotel armchairs that smelled of cigarette smoke. I discovered that Tommy shared my aversion to the loud music that so many family-friendly restaurants feel it necessary to play. And I watched as, in the nastiest of all the hotels we stayed in, he rolled from his back to his belly for the first time. It would be the first of many milestones that I would mark in a place other than my home.

My very first trip as a new mom: up the street to see the neighbors.

THE WHAT
AND WHY
OF FAMILY
TRAVEL

What You'll Learn From this Book

This book will prepare you to successfully travel with your family. There are many things you can do to make it easier to travel with kids of all ages, and these pages provide tips about planning, packing, preparing your kids to travel, and executing your trip like a pro. You'll discover how to live like a local on the road, how to make the most of cultural institutions, and what to do when things don't go quite as you planned. Much of the advice here is what I would give to any traveler, family or otherwise, adapted and adjusted to accommodate picky palates, short attention spans, and the need for daily playground time.

I'll also inspire you to just get out and go with your children, whether your trip takes you around the globe or around the block.

To me, travel is as much a state of mind as it is the action of going somewhere. It's thinking about the world and engaging with it, whether by taking a long plane ride or visiting that new museum in the next town.

I like to think it was Tommy's good example that gave me courage and stamina for all of the travel we did during the first two years of his life. He rarely complained and was always curious and enthusiastic. When his brother, Teddy came along a few years later it seemed completely natural that we would continue to travel. And so we did.

The reality is that it takes initiative to be a traveling parent. It takes action. It takes a willingness to step outside your comfort zone. If you are North American, you will have to challenge cultural assumptions that say it's more important to have 'stuff' than experiences, and that very young children should be utterly committed to a long list of activities that keep them at home.

But challenging these assumptions is a worthwhile thing to do. Travel may be less glamorous, more work-intensive, and sometimes more costly with children than without, but it is also more deliberate and meaningful.

A Year on the Road With a Toddler

With a few trial road trips under our belt, Matt and I were emboldened to try something even more ambitious. Tommy's first birthday cake was shaped like a suitcase, and just days after his party we sold our house, stored our possessions, and left for a year on the road.

'A year on the road.' The phrase had a romantic, carefree sound to it. Freedom like the beatniks had, only without the drugs, multiple lovers and broken-down cars. In my mind, I saw a year free from the obligations of home ownership, work, and social and volunteer commitments. There would be no need to think too hard, no pressure to contribute, no guilt. There would be just the three of us, and whatever we could fit in the car. It seemed very Zen: free, simple, balanced. After our successful foray into road trips with a baby, how hard could it be to travel with a toddler?

The minute we left, I realized I was on a collision course with reality. No matter how flexible you tell yourself your kid is, trying to negotiate different locations in the company of someone who requires food and/or sleep every two hours is challenging. The first day of our trip was one of the worst of our lives. Conversely the last day of the trip was one of the best, and we were sad to see the adventure end.

During our time on the road, I learned how to get by without any child-proofing whatsoever, how to keep toys to a manageable minimum, how to eat out with a toddler. I also discovered how easy it was to live without anything other than our most basic possessions for a year, how to introduce myself to strangers so that Tommy would have friends, and how to pack so the most critical items were always accessible.

To see my reward for all this effort I need go no further than my collection of photographs. There's Tommy playing with a small green plastic car at the top of Castel Sant'Angelo in Rome; then there's him riding on a Swan Boat in Boston's Public Garden; contemplating both the Atlantic and Pacific Oceans; playing with distant aunts, uncles, and grandparents; and Tommy and some new friends sitting in the miniature train at Travel Town in Los Angeles. When it came to that year on the road, I was richly rewarded for all my efforts with experiences that I will treasure forever.

Can you tell that Tommy was unhappy riding the Swan Boat in Boston? All he wanted to do was stick his hands in the water.

What is Family Travel?

Before we look at why you should travel with your family or how to go about it, let's answer an even more basic question. What is family travel?

Teddy admiring the Gulf of Mexico sunset in Fort Myers, Florida.

This is important because many families get locked into the idea that there is only one kind of travel that will work for them because children are involved. But there are as many different kinds of trips to take as there are families, and at different points in your family life, you're likely to approach travel in different ways. Ideally, within any given year, you'll find opportunities to try different types of family travel, even if you only get two weeks of vacation time.

Over the past decade, I've been a traveler of many different stripes: the mother of an infant looking to get out of the house; a road-trip warrior headed to see grandma and other relatives; a luxury traveler reveling in resort amenities; a city traveler soaking up culture with my kids; a cyclist and hiker hitting the bike path and mountain trail with my children; and, an extended traveler with no fixed address.

Let's begin by looking at some of your travel options, always remembering that your main goal is to explore the world with your family.

Day Trips

A great way to ease yourself into family travel is to take trips that are a short drive from your home, perhaps even to the next town. Visiting a museum or local attraction that you've never seen before, trying a different kind of cuisine at a new restaurant, or going for a short hike are all ways to experience 'travel' while still putting your child to bed in his or her own room.

Day trips are especially important for new parents as a way to acclimate both themselves and their children to longer adventures. If you've never tried to do more than run errands with your baby, a day trip presents a great opportunity to ease yourself into travel, and learn what you enjoy doing with your child and how to handle the inevitable bumps along the road.

Weekend Getaways

It's amazing how much even one night away can change your perspective, rejuvenate you, and give you a sense that you've had some meaningful family time.

You don't have to go far or have elaborate plans to enjoy a weekend away. A visit to a fun roadside attraction, followed by a few hours at a beloved museum you've been to many times before, can be all you have on the agenda. Simply spending a night in a hotel is exciting and fun for kids. They love the little bottles of shampoo, watching TV in bed and access to an indoor pool. Many hotels that serve business travelers during the week are eager to fill up with families on the weekend, so you can often find package deals for adjoining rooms or discounted rates for suites.

Trips to See Grandma

Visiting far-flung family or friends is another wonderful way to introduce your children to travel, with the added bonus that you may have some built-in help or babysitters. Many families (my own included) return to the same destination year after year because grandparents live there.

Tommy playing miniature golf in Franklin Square, Philadelphia, where the holes are decorated with replicas of city monuments.

Cruises, Resorts, or Guided Tours

These types of trips can be luxurious or modest. The unique feature they share is that decisions have, for the most part, been made in advance. You know where you will stay, eat, and go, as well as what you will do when you get there. There's nothing wrong with taking an 'easy' vacation like this (I use quotation marks because nothing will stop your children from getting sick, staying up all night, teething, complaining, or doing any of the many things that make travel challenging). Just don't limit yourself to organized trips or you will miss out on the opportunity for some wonderful experiences that come only from dipping your toes into more independent family travel.

City Travel

What is ideal about visiting cities pretty much anywhere in the world is that they offer a built-in menu of activities, parks, markets, and street life. Cities are also often easier to navigate with children, offering transportation options such as subways and buses that don't require car seats, and ready access to prepared food, pharmacies, toy and book stores, and public bathrooms.

Outdoor Adventure Travel

If you are someone who likes to get outside, becoming a parent doesn't mean you can't take adventurous trips anymore. With some planning, and an acknowledgement of your kids' limitations, all things are possible. From local trail systems and nature walks to state parks and ski areas, there are numerous opportunities for you to get your family into nature.

Gear companies offer equipment like backpack carriers and bike trailers that make getting outside with kids possible. If a family camping trip doesn't sound like much fun, you'll find that there are options such as lodges and cabins in many national parks.

Extended Travel

Think you can't take more than two weeks to travel? You might be surprised to learn how many families have figured out how to take a sabbatical from their lives to hit the road. The benefits of extended travel are numerous – time together as a family when your children are young, the opportunity to truly immerse your family in the culture of a new place, and the kind of learning that only comes with experience. Longer family trips take some serious financial and logistical planning, especially once children are school age, but they are an investment in your family that will pay dividends for years to come.

As you can see, there is not really a 'right' way to travel with your family – rather, there are as many choices as you and your children have interests. And within each category, there are myriad options to fit your budget and inclinations.

"*I left home in July 2011 with a picky eater and a boy who was so shy with strangers that he'd hide behind his brother when they approached. I came home a year later, after visiting 29 countries, with two boys who are much more comfortable in the world. The picky eater now asks if we can have curry at home; the shy kid is the neighborhood ringleader. My boys found themselves out there, free from what their peers might think, and without the comfort of knowing how to avoid a dish or who would speak for them.***"*

Heather Greenwood Davis, founder of
Globetrotting Mama (globetrottingmama.com)

Why Travel With Your Family?

If you look at this list of different types of family travel and think "Great! Sign me up!" then you can probably skip this chapter and just head for Section 2. But if you are feeling a bit weak in the knees and worrying that maybe this isn't the book for you, take heart! I've got many wonderful reasons why you should go to all this trouble.

Traveling with kids will help make you a better parent. In fact, it will make you a better person. Why? Because family travel requires so many different things of you. To travel well with kids you have to plan well and make sure you are prepared for all possible contingencies. When circumstances force you to abandon your carefully made plans, you have to be flexible enough to make changes on the fly and find new solutions. You must be patient during trying situations and continually think about someone other than yourself. And when you completely miss the mark you have to be able to laugh at yourself and keep on moving.

Tommy playing in a fountain in the Boboli Gardens in Florence, Italy.

Children ask questions. When you venture into the world with kids, you'll find they bring their own perspective and point of view, which is going to be fresher and more curious than yours. I can't tell you how many times I've gone to museums with my children and spent time looking at exhibits I would have completely passed by if left to my own devices – this has proved as true in the Louvre as in the tiny local history museum in Sayner, Wisconsin.

Children's curiosity and need for engagement will make experiences feel like grand adventures even when they aren't new or initially interesting to you. Aspects of travel that adults take for granted, such as staying in a hotel or visiting a park, are revealed in a completely new light because children enjoy them so much. Children don't rank their experiences in order of importance, so seeing the Eiffel Tower for the first time, or noticing a fat chartreuse caterpillar crossing your hiking trail, are both instances of absolute magic. In a way, traveling with kids allows you to live life on the same terms as a child – moment to moment, completely in the present, with little thought for what came before or what will come next.

Travel prioritizes experience over things. After one of our summer road trips, Matt tallied up our expenses and remarked that for the price of our hotel room, meals, and activities over the course of a long weekend, we could have purchased a new large-screen television.

It is true that we are lucky enough to have income left over after bills are paid and donations are made, but that income is limited, leaving the question of how best to spend it. I have never regretted spending that money on a trip.

"Family travel is good for everyone: horizons are expanded, lessons about patience and flexibility are learned, and there's a distinctly different level of mindfulness in togetherness that can be experienced when you're not surrounded by the demands of everyday life," says Christine Koh, co-author of *Minimalist Parenting: Enjoy Modern Family Life More By Doing Less.* "The trip doesn't need to be over-the-top expensive or the itinerary complicated; in fact, the less time you spend building the itinerary, the more time you'll have to simply relax and have fun. Stuff is fleeting, but memories last forever."

Teddy listening and learning about music around the world at the Musical Instrument Museum in Phoenix, Arizona.

Travel with children offers a meaningful way to spend focused time together. As my children grow older, I become more aware of just how precious our time is together; in just a few short years Tommy will be heading off to college. When we are at home the distractions of everyday modern life – school, homework, sports, music lessons, and church – limit the time we have to spend in quiet communion or meaningful conversation. Travel changes all that, bringing us together for days at a time. Even long car rides become opportunities to tell stories, share jokes and opinions, and to read books aloud together, creating common experiences that make us stronger as a family.

Travel exposes children to the world and to different cultures. This may seem obvious, but it bears repeating: whether going across the ocean or up the street, travel teaches children about the world outside the walls they inhabit. I have seen how this exposure makes my children more flexible and receptive to that world. They are always willing to try new things and they enter most new situations without hesitation because they assume they will be fun and interesting. Having children who are so open to new experiences, who embrace the world so vigorously, is worth the effort it takes to show them that world.

Around the World in Fifteen Minutes

Although my children have thus far been on only two continents, the benefits of our continuous and repeated travel play out in our day-to-day life all the time. One night, as my family was sitting around our table eating dinner, our conversation turned to a Cajun restaurant that was reviewed in the local newspaper. Matt and I were talking about how we wanted to go there for dinner one night.

"What's Cajun?" Tommy asked. I explained, and in the process of doing so talked about roux and gumbo and beignets and New Orleans. It was mutually agreed that we should go there as a family. "Actually, I want to take an entire trip across the southern United States," Matt said, "Starting in Williamsburg, and then going to Charleston and Savannah before heading west."

This idea was met by enthusiasm, and then Tommy said, "You know where else we should go? San Francisco!" It was then decided that we should also take a tour of the Pacific Northwest, heading up the coast from the Bay area to visit Portland and Seattle, maybe even flying up to Vancouver from there.

"Oh, and you know where I really want to go?" I asked. "Australia! And while we're on our way there, why don't we stop in Hawaii and do some hiking? And maybe head from there up into Asia and see Thailand and go to India?" Tommy and Teddy both thought this was a swell idea, especially when we decided we'd follow up with a stop in South Africa to go on safari, then maybe go back to Paris before coming home.

And so it was that in the space of fifteen minutes of conversation, we had circumnavigated the globe. When my children hear about a new place, their response is to ask, "When can we go? What will we see there? Who will we meet?"

I have a hope deep in my heart that all of our adventuring will encourage my children to take time to travel before they have commitments or mortgages or children themselves. When I picture them as young adults, I see them scruffy and sandaled, carrying backpacks, sleeping on friends' floors, and meeting new people wherever they go. I want them to miss trains, go for days without showers, and grow beards so that I don't even recognize them. I want them to climb mountains. I want them to explore many different foods, cultures, and landscapes. I want them to experience the limits brought on by fear and fatigue, but also the absolute freedom of having no set agenda and no one to report to.

I know that traveling with them now makes this more likely to happen, so I guess you could call family travel my not-so-secret parenting agenda.

BEFORE YOU GO: HOW TO PLAN YOUR TRIP

Learning Why I Needed a Plan

When Matt and I left for our year of travel with one-year-old Tommy, we arrived in Boston on our first day to discover that the 'luxury furnished apartment' we had rented was, in fact, down at heel and in a building full of students.

The landlord greeted us at the door, handing me a business card with office and cell phone numbers on it. "For emergencies," he said, smiling. I tried not to imagine what kind of emergencies might require his assistance, since he looked like he wouldn't have the stamina to bail himself out of a bathtub.

The first thing I saw to the immediate left of the apartment's door was a wide opening leading to a steep set of stairs. They were unfinished and dirty and descended to what seemed to be a basement door. We had no safety gate – it hadn't fitted in our car. Tommy had learned to walk the previous week.

The landlord showed us the apartment mostly with vague gestures, quickly opening and closing cabinets and doors. Despite it being June, he was intent on displaying the properties of the gas fireplace. He made no mention of air conditioning, which would later prove to be a calculated omission since, as we discovered on the next 90-degree day, it didn't work.

Released from Matt's arms, Tommy was thumping happily across the wood floor. I glanced in the kitchen cabinets and saw stacks of saucers, but only one pot. A cigarette butt sat in the bottom of the garbage can. In the narrow bathroom, a forlorn ponytail holder hung on a hook in the shower, and the bathmat was dirty.

Before I really had a chance to voice any objections, the landlord's cell phone rang and he disappeared without saying goodbye. At that moment, I discovered a note stuck to the apartment's phone indicating there wouldn't be service for four days. Two weeks later, it still wasn't working, and Matt and I had been kept up until dawn every night by the parties in the apartment above ours.

We all survived that experience and can even laugh about it now, but it was a quick education in the importance of planning well when traveling with kids. I hadn't vetted the apartment carefully enough, hadn't asked for a reference or really even seen many pictures of it, relying entirely on the description that appeared on a locator service website which claimed it was 'great temporary housing for professionals and families'. Never again would I walk quite so blindly into a travel experience with my children.

Choosing a Destination

Before you begin your planning for any trip, the first thing you need to decide is where to go.

When making this decision, remember that you know your family better than anyone else. Don't feel that there are certain trips you 'should' take just because other families you know have done so.

My entire family loves to ski, so this trip to Northstar Resort near Lake Tahoe, California was fun for all of us.

If your kids really don't like museums, planning to visit Washington, DC, may not be your best bet. My children don't have a good time at amusement parks, so I usually avoid them. On the other hand, there's nothing wrong with getting outside your comfort zone, and challenging yourself and your family to experience something new.

Start by thinking of the type of trip you'd like to take. I outlined some of the options for family travel earlier. Consider them, and then ask yourself the following questions:

What is my budget in both money and time? Be realistic about how much money you want to spend, and whether or not you can afford to take time off work or away from school. There's nothing wrong with doing a series of long weekend trips as opposed to one longer trip, if that is what fits with your family's schedule and means. If that's the case, you might want to factor in the amount of time it takes you to get to the destination, and choose places to visit that are closer to home, so your vacation time isn't eaten up en route.

Another thing to consider is whether the time you have available for your trip coincides with a given destination's busy season when prices will be high and attractions will be crowded.

For most destinations, school holidays and the busier seasons are one and the same, so if you have younger children or the ability to pull your children out of school, you might travel at times when everyone else is staying home.

Not every trip has to be a 'dream vacation'. I travel frequently with my kids and can't afford to go to another continent every time I want to get away. I've found that some of our best trips have been to destinations I only considered because they happened to be within driving distance of our home.

What are my goals? Different destinations offer different advantages. Are you looking to relax and spend lots of quality family time together? Or are you primarily interested in exposing your children to new cultures and educational experiences? It's not that you can't do both on a given trip, but your ability to do so will be dependent on your time and resources.

Resort vacations, no matter what the location, tend to offer concentrated family time, and the opportunity for everyone to relax without thinking too hard. City trips are more challenging and usually involve interesting cultural experiences, plus the excitement (and exhaustion) that comes from riding public transportation or hustling down crowded sidewalks.

Traveling can be tiring, even in such a beautiful place as Versailles.

You might also plan your travel around a seasonal activity like skiing or camping. Since you have less control over when you can do these things, and since ski areas and campgrounds tend to be busy at the times when snow and sun are available, planning well in advance is advisable.

How many places should we visit during a given trip? I have a conservative philosophy about this and tend to prefer 'slower travel' with my kids. That means I rarely plan fewer than two full days in any one location. It can be tricky to balance the desire to 'see everything' (especially when you've traveled far from home) with the reality that children won't do well when you cram too much into each day of your trip. My approach is to treat every place my family visits as if we'll be back, whether or not that is actually true.

Are there activities that everyone in my family will enjoy? When thinking about a given destination, ask yourself whether there are age-appropriate things for every member of your family. These requirements will change as your children grow.

Not every place you visit has to please everyone in your family, especially if you have children of varying ages and interests. But there should be at least one thing on the agenda planned especially for each person on the trip.

Dressing up in period costume made a visit to Colonial Williamsburg fun even for Teddy, the youngest member of my family.

Should you take a cruise or go on a tour? If the idea of traveling independently with your kids overwhelms you, or you want to cover a lot of territory in a short period of time, a cruise or packaged tour may be your best option for family travel. Both tours and cruises offer you the chance to travel without having to create your own itinerary. If you choose one that is family-friendly, you will find amenities that both you and your kids will enjoy, staff who are prepared to help you with your children, and the company of other families with kids.

I focus more on independent family travel, but you will find websites to help you choose cruises or packaged tours in the 'Resources' section at the end of the book.

"My kids have slowed me down from the rat race I was running for far too long. We are still able to see a lot when we visit a new place, but now I actually see it. Instead of checking one more sight off a list, I sit down, talk to them about it, learn what they love, have the time to figure out what I love, and really absorb why this spot is worth checking out."

Keryn Means, founder of Walking on Travels (walkingontravels.com)

Choosing a Hotel or Resort

Once you've decided where you want to go, the next step is choosing where you'll stay. Since lodging is often a considerable part of your vacation expense, choosing it bears some careful thought. This is especially true when traveling with children, because if they are uncomfortable or unhappy you are likely to be so as well.

When it comes to hotels and resorts your choices are numerous and varied. There are chain hotels off the highway that feature convenience as the only real amenity, and there are resorts where you'll find everything from water parks to horseback riding to mini golf. Some hotels offer kids club programs and babysitting so that the grown-ups can get in some kid-free time; others have family movie or game nights that encourage you to play with your children.

You can't go wrong choosing a hotel with a pool. And one that has a water park? Even better.

Finding the Right Hotel

A great starting point for your research is to ask people you know where they've stayed. Anne Taylor Hartzell, publisher of the blog Hip Travel Mama suggests reaching out to your friends and social networks both at home and online. "Ask what hotels and resorts they love and why," she says.

Kara Williams, freelance writer and co-publisher of The Vacation Gals also recommends checking review sites before choosing a hotel or resort. "I read recent TripAdvisor reviews before I book any hotel," she says, "Although, I do take them with a grain of salt. The hotel doesn't have to be the best in the destination (that is, ranking #1), but if I can find some families who had an enjoyable stay there in the last year or two, I feel more comfortable booking."

Like the other aspects of your trip, what makes a hotel right for you is dependent on your family's needs. With that said, there are a few things to look for:

Location, location, location. Children simultaneously resent travel time and can require a lot of gear. If you're visiting the beach or skiing, the closer you can be to the shore or slopes, the better off you'll be. In a city, look for a hotel that is either near the things you want to see or within an easy walk to public transportation.

"We're always willing to pay more to be within walking distance to a city's main attractions and entertainment," says Nicole Wears, co-founder with her husband Cam of the blog Traveling Canucks. "Traveling with an infant or toddler is no easy task, nor is trying to figure out a city's public transportation with a stroller. We prefer to skip transit and instead stay right in the action. It costs more, but allows us to avoid unnecessary headaches. Plus, it allows us to be close to our hotel if our son gets cranky and needs a nap."

Some extra space. I have learned over years of hotel stays that children will fall asleep with the light on, and that it's not necessary when renting a single room to cower in the bathroom with a plastic cup of wine until they pass out.

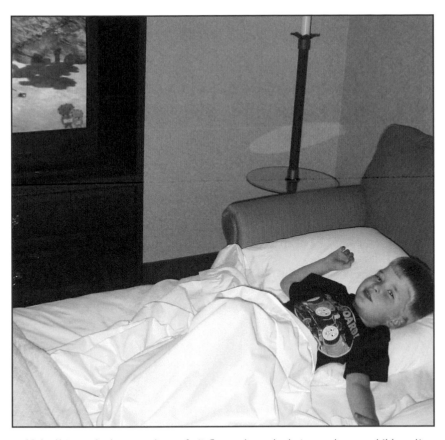

Teddy had his own bed, a TV, and some fruit-flavored cereal: what more does any child need in a hotel room?

Many hotels offer slightly larger rooms for families, some with a sofa next to the sleeping area. There may be no wall between you and the kids, but when you aren't sitting on the bed next to theirs while you're trying to get them to fall asleep, it creates some psychological space. If you've got more than three kids, you'll probably want to look at hotels that offer adjoining rooms.

Small hotel rooms can also work under certain circumstances. All four members of my family once stayed in a tiny room in a bed and breakfast hotel (B&B) in Windsor, England, that was perfect because it had a bunk bed for the boys. The owners (who had a large family themselves) allowed Matt and me to bring our computers to the breakfast room after we put the children to bed, which meant we didn't feel overly crowded or have to go to bed at seven o'clock.

On-site breakfast. My children wake up hungry, and always have. When I don't have my own kitchen, it is imperative that I have access to sustenance first thing in the morning. A basic chain hotel breakfast is just fine – often my kids will eat it and then we'll go out for a better meal at a restaurant later in the morning – but I really love hotels that offer generous, cooked-to-order breakfasts. These can carry us through whatever activities I have planned early in the day.

A kitchenette, or, at the very least, a small refrigerator. You may not plan to cook on your trip, but you will want to have a place to chill juice boxes or keep picnic items cold.

Resort credits. If you are staying in a resort, check the website to see if credits are offered as part of the cost of your room, says Hartzell. These credits are included in the price of your room package and may cover meals for your children, resort activities like tennis or golf, or even spa treatments for you.

Benefits of Hotels and Resorts

One of the advantages of staying in a hotel or at a resort is that you always have access to someone who can solve your problems or answer your questions. This can be especially helpful if you have very young children who need more constant care, or if you are visiting a country where you don't speak the language and need help calling restaurants or attractions.

Carol Cain, founder and publisher of Girl Gone Travel says that good customer service and friendly staff are key when she is staying at a hotel or resort. "When you are traveling, especially with kids, you can adjust to and forgive many things, including small rooms, not enough beds, no television, no connecting rooms, or only one tiny bathroom. But I can't think of any situation where top-notch customer service doesn't win every time."

The Hotel Monaco in Baltimore offers kid-sized bathrobes, which Teddy loved.

A hotel or resort doesn't have to be large or super luxurious to have these advantages. The owners of a small B&B in Bucks County, Pennsylvania provided us with homemade brownies and great restaurant recommendations before giving us a fascinating tour of the tunnel beneath their property that is thought to have been part of the Underground Railroad.

A hotel can also be part of your family's cultural experience. In the western United States, dude ranch resorts allow guests to ride the range with real cowboys. You might also use a hotel to enter into the history of a place. Across Europe you can stay in hotels that are former castles, villas, or monastaries.

" *In Tokyo, we stayed in a tatami room at a traditional ryokan where we slept on futons on the floor. The deep tub in the bathroom was the size of a small swimming pool and was controlled by an elaborate panel of buttons. The room was simple, comfortable, and we could push the futons together to make one large bed for the four of us. Futons on tatami mats, it turns out, are much more comfortable than the pullout futons in the United States.* **"**

Ashley Steel and Bill Richards, authors of *Family on the Loose: The Art of Traveling with Kids*

Saving Money on Hotels and Resorts

Hotels and resorts often offer package deals that include meals or activities as part of your stay. Although packages can sometimes save you money, you should check them carefully, says Jessica Bowers, founder and publisher of the blog Suitcases and Sippy Cups. "Package deals can be a great money saver if you are sure you are going to take advantage of all the elements," she says. "If the package includes extras that you don't need, you may be better off buying the elements individually. Do a little quick math before you book."

If you stay in a chain hotel of any variety, check to see if they offer a loyalty program before you arrive. Usually these are free, and offer benefits like free coffee and juice in the morning, perks for kids like cookies at check in, and even upgrades to larger rooms.

"I love seeing a new place through my daughters' eyes. Most of the time, they get me to focus on an aspect of a place that I wouldn't otherwise notice. Maybe it's a flower. Maybe it's a doorway. Whatever it is, they see the world in a different way, and that way often helps to open my mind."

Matt Villano, founder of Wandering Pod (wanderingpod.com)

Choosing a Vacation Rental

Many of the same family-friendly criteria apply to vacation rentals as to hotels – you're looking for location, space, and amenities such as pools and game rooms. You'll also want to check with previous renters to find out how loud any vacation rental is and whether other families tend to stay in the vicinity. Vacation rentals are a great bet when you will be staying in one place with kids for more than five days. Although you trade the convenience of having an on-site concierge, you make up for that in the extra space, the ability to cook meals and do laundry, and the chance to live like a local.

There are a number of websites and agencies that will help you find vacation rentals, some of them high end, others more economical. I have often used HomeAway or Vacation Rentals By Owner, both in the United States and abroad, and have never had a bad experience. In resort communities such as ski areas or beach towns, there are usually local real estate agents who can help you if you prefer the personal touch. When choosing a vacation rental, make sure you do the following:

Check references. Since that first negative experience, I always ask to be connected with someone (preferably someone with kids) who has rented the apartment or condo before. If possible, I speak to both the person renting the apartment and the referee on the phone.

Review the rental terms carefully. By familiarizing yourself with the terms, you will know exactly what is expected of you and what you will be getting. Sometimes there may be an extra cleaning fee payable when you check out, or you may be required to run the dishwasher and strip the beds before you leave.

Know how much you are expected to pay upfront. I once neglected to confirm this when renting in London and showed up with insufficient amounts of British currency. The rental agent was nice about it, but it would have been better to arrive prepared to pay the amount that was expected of me.

Camping With Kids

Camping can be one of the most economical ways to go on a family vacation. Amy Whitley, founder of Pit Stops for Kids and editor at the family travel site Trekaroo, has camped extensively with her own children in everything from crowded campgrounds to backwoods cabins. Whitley offers the following suggestions for families interested in tent or cabin camping:

Choosing a tent or cabin campground. State and national park campgrounds offer more isolated and scenic tent camping sites than most private campgrounds. Look for campgrounds with a healthy ratio of tent and recreational vehicle (RV) spots to ensure that tent campers aren't just pushed to the fringes of an RV-heavy park.

Pick a site that is not next door to, but is within easy walking distance of, bathrooms. Picnic tables and fire pits are a must for campground camping, and shade is a plus.

If you don't want to travel with tents and other camping essentials, then look for campgrounds offering on-site cabins or yurts. These are affordable, sleep five to six people, and provide beds and shelter (and sometimes kitchens).

If you are looking for activities on your camping trip, pick national park campgrounds with evening campfire programs on-site. Want some seclusion? Opt for campgrounds housing wildlife sanctuaries. These usually maintain only a handful of sites (often walk-in tent camping) and are extremely quiet and solitary for the same price as more crowded campgrounds. Campgrounds with only basic amenities, such as pit toilets, will also be quieter.

Kids love sleeping in a tent, but be warned – they may wake up very early.

For community, services, and a lively atmosphere choose private campgrounds with plenty of amenities (such as pools or playgrounds) or state or national park campgrounds with visitor centers on-site.

When to book a campsite. National and state park campgrounds are very popular during summer months, so it's important to start planning for a summer trip as early as six months ahead.

And don't forget about wilderness permits. These are often a requirement for campers looking to explore a national park's backcountry wilderness. Call the park's wilderness office at least six months prior to the trip date, and be aware that some parks use a lottery system.

Tips for RV travel. Another way to camp with kids is in an RV. Jessica Bowers of Suitcases and Sippy Cups traveled around the eastern United States for three months in an RV with her four sons and offers these tips.

- Many sites cater towards retired or year-round guests, and may not readily welcome children – call ahead to ask.
- Choosing a campsite with posted quiet hours is the best way to ensure you will camp in a site that is family friendly.
- Not all RV parks are in heavily treed areas. Many sites are wide, bare parking lots that offer little shade or other natural areas. These types of sites are ideal for parking a large RV, but can take away from the relaxed, outdoor atmosphere.
- Does the campsite have basic electric, water, and sewage facilities? Do you need full hookups, and if full hookups are not available, are there plenty of restroom and shower facilities? Laundry can also be important if you are traveling long-term. Check to see that washing machines are available and in working order. Some campgrounds have on-site change machines and detergent dispensers, and others provide only washers and dryers. Call ahead to be prepared with the proper supplies.
- Ask about food and supply options, especially if you are camping in a remote area. A campsite with a general store that carries basic camping and RV supplies is ideal. Many campsites also offer propane-refilling stations.

- Many campsites have gates that are locked each evening to add extra security. Determine if the office is open 24 hours a day, or if there is a number to call in case of emergency.

You will find websites to help you choose a campsite for both tent and RV camping in the 'Resources' section.

Planning Your Transportation

One of the biggest challenges of traveling with kids is the actual travel. It's become increasingly difficult to find affordable airline tickets and nonstop flights, and many airlines now charge an extra fee to guarantee your family is seated together. Driving is no easier; more cars on the road mean traffic congestion, and gas prices are high.

How you get to your destination will depend on where you are going. If you have a choice between driving and flying, you should consider whether you will need a car when you arrive, how much gas and tolls will cost, what the costs of parking a vehicle are (if any), and how much time it will take you to get there.

Planning flights. If you will be flying, your best bet for finding a deal is to set up some online fare alerts well in advance of your trip. Websites such as Airfarewatchdog and FareCompare allow you to enter your route and the dates you're interested in; you'll receive email alerts when your routes go on sale. The trick here is to cast as wide a net as possible. If you have any flexibility in your dates or your departure or arrival airport, you're more likely to find deals.

If you don't want to clutter up your inbox, create a separate email account for these emails; you can also use that address to sign up for hotel and car rental deal alerts.

Another way to save money on airline tickets is to sign up for a credit card that accrues miles or points as you use it. If you put all of your major expenses on one card, you will accumulate miles fairly quickly. I have also used my miles to rent cars or find discounted hotel rooms.

A special consideration when flying with kids is making the trip as easy as possible, even if the plane tickets are more expensive. When flying with young children, it is worth sacrificing a few days of a trip, or staying in a less expensive hotel, in order to have nonstop flights that head directly to your destination. Flight delays can create real headaches when you have connecting flights, and airlines are increasingly booking connecting flights that are simply too close for comfort.

Overnight red-eye flights with children are always a good bet, especially when going from west to east. Children are much more likely to fall asleep on a red-eye flight than one during the day. I've always booked flights like this on our trips to Europe, and we stay awake as long as possible during that first day and, after an early bedtime, we're ready to go the next morning with relatively little jet lag.

One last thing to remember is to consider other options for travel, including trains and buses, which offer the same benefits as flying (the ability to move around in transit, the fact that no parent has to drive) without the hassle of security or airline delays.

Planning road trips. When my children were little, I usually planned our road trips so that we didn't spend more than five or six hours per day in the car. For longer drives, I would include the cost of a hotel with a pool in our travel budget, and we'd stop and spend the night en route. This may have added time and expense to the trip, but it also made things more relaxed and fun.

Now that my children are older, we can easily drive for ten to 12 hours without a complaint from either of them. I like to think that's because I made car travel fun, and not too much of an endurance test, when they were young.

A Detour Can Be Your Friend

We were on the last leg of the last day of a three-week driving trip that had taken us around the Midwestern United States in a huge loop. After many hours in the car, we had crossed from West Virginia into Maryland when traffic suddenly came to a complete stop for 45 minutes because of a serious accident. Once it started moving, we were going at a pace of about ten miles an hour. It was late afternoon and we'd been in the car since eight o'clock in the morning.

I consulted our atlas, realized how far from home we still were, and made a command decision: we would get off the interstate, drive north into Pennsylvania, and take the two-lane Route 30 across the state through Gettysburg to Lancaster. We would then be in familiar territory as we knew the back roads back to Delaware. Here's what ensued:

We drove through the lovely rolling hills of central-western Pennsylvania, which was golden in the sun, while the kids napped because the car was moving.

Although we had to slow down to 30 miles per hour through any number of small towns, we encountered virtually no traffic anywhere and made decent time.

At the exact moment when all of us wanted dinner, we were driving through the fields that surround Gettysburg and happened upon a local brewpub that served nutritious kids' meals and delicious beer.

The last hour of our trip was spent not in tears and recrimination, but with giddy, slap-happy kids who shrieked and laughed and generally enjoyed the naughty feeling of being up late and out after dark.

How to Create an Itinerary

Traveling with kids makes you less nimble, which means that it's best to make detailed lists of what you will do on each day of your trip. You don't have to plan every moment of your trip, however, and any plan you make should be more of a guide than a set of step-by-step instructions. Here are my tips for creating an itinerary:

- Start by making a list of everything you think you'd like to do. If your children are old enough, involve them in this part of the process simply by sharing the list and asking for their feedback.

- Map out how many days you have, making ample accommodation for travel time, and remember you may not want to do much on the day when you arrive.

- Plan a maximum of two 'anchor' activities per day, and then whittle down your master list accordingly.

- Case out the neighborhood around any attraction or museum you'll be visiting. Are there playgrounds, places to get ice cream, or bookstores? If you're going on a hike, will you pass a family-friendly farm with a petting zoo on the way to and from the parking area? Local parenting magazines, many of which now have websites, can be a great resource for finding fun things to do.

- Mix it up – day after day of museum visits isn't going to be fun even if your kids really like museums.

- Double-check opening and closing times.

- When possible, buy tickets in advance – if that's not possible, factor waiting time into your plans. On occasion, I've found it a good idea to pay a premium to avoid monstrous lines. At the London Eye, for example, I purchased fast-track tickets that not only helped us jump to the front of the line, they also gave the boys a backpack with a small pair of binoculars and some other souvenirs. Given that the end point of the entrance line was two hours back on the day that we visited, it was definitely worth the extra money.

- Make sure you have alternate indoor plans for weather-dependent activities.

An important thing to remember when you are crafting your itinerary is that downtime is a critical part of traveling with kids. Children of all ages need unstructured time to recharge their mental and physical batteries. Build time into each day to just hang out at a park or your hotel, even if your kids no longer take naps.

When you sit down to create your itinerary, take time to make sure your travel documentation is in order. Children need new passports more often than adults, so you'll want to leave yourself plenty of time to get new ones if necessary. If you are a parent traveling without your children's other parent, you will need a notarized note of permission to take them out of the country. If they will need immunizations, you'll want to schedule those appointments as well (I talk more about safety considerations and planning in the 'Safety on the Road' chapter).

Packing for a Family

I haven't always been a savvy packer. For many years, having small children masked this sad fact. We hauled an enormous duffle bag with us on planes, and filled our car to bursting on road trips. It's really not fair to blame the children; our luggage was stuffed with toys, booster seats, and diapers, but it also held numerous pairs of my shoes and full-sized bottles of shampoo.

The advent of airline fees for luggage – and my cover being blown once my kids didn't need so much gear – means I've had to change my ways. In spite of my love of hair products and shoes, in July of 2010 my family managed to travel for two weeks in England without checking a single bag on the plane. Here are my tips for packing light when traveling with kids.

Decide what you really need. Some good questions to ask yourself when deciding what to bring on a trip include: How many of this item will I use? Is this something I can reasonably buy when I get there? Will I actually use or wear this? Be honest and ruthless.

Create a packing list of essential items that you use every time you travel. What goes on the list will change over time – you may start with diapers and binkies and move onto allergy medications and extra pairs of glasses as your kids grow. Having a prepared list means less thought when it comes time to pack, and less chance you will forget something critical.

Make sure you have the right suitcases. Matt and I received luggage as a wedding gift and we used those same suitcases – heavy, large, and coming apart at the seams – for many years after we had children. Finally, I realized how sick I was of pulling out those monster suitcases every time we traveled, and went to a discount store to buy small, lightweight, wheeled bags. Each boy got his own suitcase and, for the most part, is now responsible for handling his own luggage.

I never had two children in a stroller at the same time. If that is not the case for you, I recommend traveling with a double stroller that folds up, and investing in two small wheeled bags and two bags without wheels that can slip over those suitcases' handles. One adult can push children and diaper bags, while the other person can pull four bags.

Invest in travel size products. Most products come in smaller sizes, or you can purchase tubes and bottles that you can fill from your full-size containers.

Are you flying? Wear your heaviest clothes and shoes on the plane. It was 100-degrees Fahrenheit the day we left for England in July, but I made the boys put on their sweatpants and hoodies for the flight. I've even been known to wear three or four tops on my body as a way to transport more clothing.

Clothing you remove can serve as blankets or pillows on long flights. And, if you're like me, you're always cold on planes anyway.

Plan your trip so that you can do laundry. Make sure you have access to a washing machine at some point during your trip. My favorite approach is to rent an apartment with laundry facilities. You can also stay in a hotel that has a laundry service or scope out the laundromats in your neighborhood. Don't forget to add the cost to your budget.

Older kids can manage their own luggage on the road if you make sure they have the right suitcases.

Use the postal service. When you're staying in the same place (in your home country) for a while, and may need hiking boots or more toys than you can carry, consider shipping a box ahead of you using the postal service. Insure the contents.

Forget something? Check with your hotel. The lost and found at the resort you are visiting is likely to have everything from cell phone chargers to kid-sized sweaters.

What to do When You Can't Travel Light

On some trips, you'll need gear because you will be skiing, biking, or camping. If you're traveling by car, you'll want to invest in racks or a rooftop box. If you're flying, your best bet may be to rent equipment at your destination or if you're going on a longer domestic trip, to ship a box ahead of you.

Even if we will be renting bikes or skis, I bring along our helmets, since these are sized properly for our heads. Skiing, in particular, requires a lot of extra clothing; for this reason, I invested in a large duffle bag that holds all our ski gear in one place.

Preparing Your Kids to Travel

As soon as your children are old enough to understand that you'll be taking a trip, it's a great idea to prepare them for it. Doing so will help insure not only that they are engaged and excited about what you are doing, but it will also give you a chance to help them overcome any fears or anxieties they might have about hitting the road.

Have your kids help you plan. As I mentioned earlier, one way you can help prepare your children for travel is to involve them in the planning process. Asking them their opinions about the things you will be doing gives you a chance to talk about your destination, and why you are excited about going there. You can also pull up websites for individual museums or attractions to explore – many of these will have special online areas just for kids.

Another idea is to let each child plan one entire day of your trip from start to finish (guiding them to help keep your activity at a reasonable level, of course). Not only will your child love the planning, but when you get to that part of your trip, he or she will also have the chance to assume total ownership of it. You might even let your child be in charge of the camera to document his or her special day.

Do some recon. My children love maps, so before we go somewhere new I get out an atlas and we'll explore the destination – starting with where it is in the world, and then drilling down to the individual continent and country. We will also explore individual city maps, either in print or online. If we're heading to a location we've visited before, we'll take a look at photos and talk about them.

Read all about it. Books are another way to introduce children to the places you will be visiting; I always head for the library to see what I can find both in the fiction and nonfiction section. Reading stories set in that location can really bring your destination to life. Once there, you can look for sites that were mentioned in the book.

Introduce the language. If your travel will include destinations where a new language is spoken, introduce some simple phrases – greetings, 'please', and 'thank you' are good places to begin. You might also cook food from the region or visit restaurants that serve it.

And finally, encourage your children to ask questions about the trip and take the time to answer them, doing some additional research if necessary. Part of the fun of traveling is anticipating your trip; by talking to your children and learning about a new place together, you extend the pleasure of the journey.

Before we visited Independence Hall in Philadelphia, Tommy read all about American history.

"*Traveling in Bhutan was my favorite part of the year-long, round-the-world trip I took with my two sons. Initially, I was concerned that the kids would be completely disinterested in the scheduled visits to multiple religious sites. Instead, they embraced the whole experience and were completely captivated by the statues, prayer wheels, and ceremonial offerings.*

At our last stop in Paro, our youngest son, Stefan (then eight) arranged a shrine in our hotel room with all the items we had picked up along the way, complete with Buddhas, incense, offering bowls, prayer beads and flags, cymbals, and bells. I know he can still recall everything from that trip."

Rainer Jenss, special correspondent,
National Geographic Intelligent Travel
(intelligenttravel.nationalgeographic.com)

ON THE ROAD: MAKING THE MOST OF YOUR TRIP

When Paris was Our Oyster

When I first went to Paris with my sons, they were three and six and I was unprepared for how enchanted both of them would be by the Eiffel Tower. I don't know why I didn't expect this: as objects go, it is utterly irresistible. Its allure lies not only in its presence, which is such a part of the Parisian landscape, but also in its absence. When you are in a part of Paris where you can't see it, you long for it, look for it, seek it out.

"There it is, Mama!" three-year-old Teddy called out triumphantly more than once. "The Eiffel Tower!" As if he alone had discovered this rare and beautiful thing.

We left the most important of visits until the last day of our two-week stay. Having received dire warnings of two-hour lines, we hustled out the door and arrived at the base of the tower about ten minutes after it opened. Although it was the beginning of July, it was blustery and none of us was dressed warmly enough. But the thrill of standing underneath the tower was enough to distract us all.

How is it possible that the tower is not a cliché? It isn't. We watched the elevators and shivered in the cool, damp breeze. Finally, it was our turn to be shepherded by the attendants, who wore the chicest grey and orange uniforms with foulards that were to die for, into an elevator.

Lest you think all we did was wax poetic, I'll hasten to let you know that while we waited in line, Teddy and Matt came up with an alternate name for the tower: the Awful Tooter. "Toot" is the polite word we taught the boys to use instead of "fart." There was much hilarity at the top as well, when Matt held Teddy and sang: "Oh look at the top of the Eiffel Tower, da dee, da dee, da dee, da doo," in a falsetto voice that would do Monty Python proud. It was very giggly up there.

The boys also really enjoyed looking for all the places we'd been during the past two weeks. "Mama, there's Sacre Coeur!" Tommy cried, pointing out the white dome in the distance.

We were up there for a good long while. Afterwards, we walked over a bridge across the river to picnic outside the Palais de Chaillot, but it was closed off in anticipation of the next week's July 14th festivities. So after snapping a few quick pictures and fending off the vendors selling Eiffel Tower key chains, we ate instead in the park on the Champ de Mars next to the tower.

After lunch, we decided that our final Parisian expedition would be for ice cream at Berthillon on the Ile Saint Louis, which we had already enjoyed several times on this trip. We made our way past Notre Dame and the crowds watching a blues band on the Pont Saint Louis, onto our magical little island. It had been dubbed 'Ice Cream Island' by the boys, who had overheard me calling the ice cream at Berthillon "the best in Paris." At some point on our trip this morphed into "the best ice cream in the world."

The sky cleared, there was no line, and we tasted sublime mint ice cream that was the essence of all that mint and cream should be. The boys also had cherry-plum ice cream, charmingly named Mirabelle.

A bride stepped out of a doorway, a sculptural white collar setting off her dark upswept hair. Church bells rang.

The boys waved to the Bateaux Mouches on the Seine, hello and good-bye. After our ice cream was gone and a few gifts were purchased it would be back to our rented apartment, and in the morning, the beginning of a long trek home. But none of us thought of that then. For that perfect moment, Paris was ours and we belonged to it, wholly.

Our first family trip to Paris was full of memorable moments.

Flying With Kids

The story of our visit to the Eiffel Tower exemplifies what I love about traveling with my children, especially the pleasure of watching their sense of wonder. But before we could have our perfect moment in Paris, we had to get there, which is often the very hardest part about traveling with kids.

Before you fly. I'm not going to sugar-coat it – flying has become a headache for everyone. My family flew four times in the year before I wrote this book, and every single one of those trips involved a problem of some variety that was not our fault. We experienced delays, cancelled flights, mechanical problems, and outright lies from gate agents at the airport.

The best thing you can do when flying with kids is prepare yourself to deal with some degree of hassle, even if that hassle is just asking someone to switch seats so that you can sit next to your six-year-old (if you can believe it, we once had someone refuse to do this).

There are a few things you can do to help make airline travel with kids go more smoothly. Start by checking in and printing your boarding passes at home. You can usually do this 24 hours in advance. Keep all your documents, including your boarding passes, confirmation numbers for hotels and rental cars, and your identification or passports in one place that you can easily access once you're at the airport.

Keep yourself informed about delays or problems. Many airlines now have smartphone applications that will send you text messages or email alerts, but my favorite tool for this purpose is the TripIt app, which will let you know well in advance if your flight time has been changed. It also saves all of your itinerary information, including confirmation numbers, in one place.

While you don't want to leave too early, give yourself plenty of time to get to the airport well before your flight so that you don't feel anxious. If you are driving to the airport, start by checking the traffic report so you will know if there will be any delays. If you have checked in online, try to arrive at the doors to the airport two hours before your flight is scheduled to depart (you will need to leave yourself more time if you have not yet checked in).

Outside the Charles de Gaulle Airport in Paris after a red-eye flight with two kids and a lot of gear.

Dealing with airport security. If you have young children, ask the agents at airport security if they have a separate family line so you can get organized without worrying about people behind you getting antsy. There are usually more agents to help in this line as well, so you'll have some assistance getting your luggage moving through the scanner.

As soon as your children are old enough to understand they will have to go through security at the airport, explain to them what will happen so they will understand the notion that their bags (possibly containing a precious toy) will be going on a conveyor belt, will disappear, and will reappear on the other side. Be prepared: everything that will need to be pulled out of bags and put into bins should be in one place, so that you can easily reach in and grab them – ideally with one hand if you've got a toddler you need to corral with the other. When I had little ones I even learned to fold up and put our umbrella stroller on the belt with one hand. Wear slip-on shoes that come on and off easily.

You are allowed to bring breast milk and formula; you are also permitted to have cooling packs to keep them fresh. Just be prepared to pull these items out and show them to the agents at security if the amounts are larger than those specified for other liquids.

Making the most of the airport. Once we have passed through security, we always make our way immediately to our gate and then encourage the kids to get their wiggles out. Many airports have play areas for younger children (apps like Gate Guru will tell you where these are located) and older kids will be happy to take a stroll to the newsstand for a pack of gum or a magazine. If you'll be flying overnight, this is a great time to have everyone brush his or her teeth. Nicole Wiltrout, founder of the blog Arrows Sent Forth, also recommends buying milk before you get on the plane if your child likes to drink it, as many airlines don't offer it as part of their beverage service.

We found a table-tennis table at the airport in Milwaukee.

Hopefully things will go smoothly, but if your flight is delayed or cancelled the best thing you can do is be your family's advocate: start politely and firmly asking the gate agents for meal vouchers and tickets on a different flight, or on a different airline, if necessary. Can't get help at the airport? Call the airline's toll free number.

Don't assume that the airline will fix your problem or offer a reasonable solution without you asking for one, even if you are traveling with little kids. Airlines in the United States are required to compensate you up to four times the value of your ticket if you are involuntarily bumped from your flight, so know your rights and be persistent. You can find more information about this at the Department of Transportation Aviation Consumer Protection website[1].

It once took my family 19 hours door-to-door to get from the East to the West Coast of the United States on a plane. The best thing you can do to help your children in situations like these is to keep as calm and cheerful as you can. By modeling good behavior, you teach them to handle these glitches in your travel plans.

Keeping kids happy on the plane. It is often the idea of the flight itself that elicits the greatest concern from parents who have not yet flown with their kids. Maybe that's because everyone has been on a plane with a baby who won't stop crying.

In fact, infants may actually be the easiest children of all to fly with. Mine usually started the flight with a snack, and then slept. Toddlers are more challenging, of course. Most of us who have travelled with young, mobile children have a story or two about a blown-out diaper, a child with an ear infection and a piercing cry, or a toddler who spent an entire transatlantic flight pacing the aisle like a caged animal, parent in tow. But we also have stories of flights when our children slept the entire time or sat happily in their seats.

Keryn Means, founder and publisher of Walking On Travels has flown many times with her toddler and infant sons – often without her husband. Her motto on planes is, "do whatever it takes to get there."

"This usually means bending the house rules. It also calls for a few special treats that only show up on airplanes," she says. "My three-year-old knows he is only allowed to have my electronic tablet on a plane, and that he can play games, watch movies or read books. The tablet is his for the duration of the flight. He also knows he will have to take breaks to eat, stretch, and go to the toilet, but other than that he is thrilled to sit with his headphones on for however long it takes to get from point A to point B."

It's great when distractions work to keep your young child happy on a plane, but when they don't, remember that any given flight, no matter how unpleasant, is of limited duration.

Wiltrout says she likes to compare flying with small children to childbirth. "I assure any new mother that it's not nearly as painful!" she says. "But, in that same sense, while it might be a little unpleasant, it ends with a wonderful outcome (your fun vacation). So just grin and bear it, and know that eventually the plane lands and you can get on to better things."

Now that my kids are older, the excitement of air travel makes it in some ways easier than a long car ride. They read, play games, and listen to music but unless the flight is turbulent, they can get up and walk around and use the bathroom. And even if modern-day air travel lacks glamour for adults, children are just happy they can watch a movie inches from their faces.

If you are looking for games you can load on your phone or tablet before you travel, the website Best Kids Apps rates hundreds of them and also lists them according to age and topic.

Traveling by Car

I've been taking road trips with my children almost since the moment they were born. Over the years we've logged hundreds of hours and thousands of miles, many of them in a small sedan, which for years was the only car we owned. Here are my tips for making sure kids stay happy in the car.

Tommy playing catch at a rest area along the Pennsylvania Turnpike.

Plan your stops in advance. Generally, our stops revolve around food – either a picnic or a meal in a local restaurant. I avoid chains, even on the interstate my favorite app for assisting with this is Local Eats. You can decide how far you'd like to drive without stopping, and then use Google to find a town with a great looking diner and a park where the kids can play. Tommy always has a set of baseball gloves in the car so he and Matt can play catch.

Keep something up your sleeve. I always stock my kids with new books, colored pencils (better than crayons in a hot car), activity books, and car games when we hit the road. But I also keep in reserve one of whatever it is that most pops my kids' corks – a comic book or even a new iPhone game – and pull it out when the joy of travel has worn thin, maybe in that unbearable last hour of the drive, which is longer than all the others combined.

Make a soundtrack for your trip that pleases everyone. Every time we have a long road trip planned, Matt and I create a themed playlist that we debut on the first day of driving. We can and do include music we already own, but we also tend to use this as an excuse to browse for songs we didn't know we wanted, which is a fun thing to do in itself.

Play some road trip games together. From 'I-Spy' to the license plate game, there are lots of ways to have fun in the car. The website KidsHealth has a fun list of road trip boredom buster ideas[2].

"My 17-year-old daughter Kayla is a travel-savvy
young woman who recently flew to Austria on her
own to attend a week-long ski camp and a month-long
engineering internship. She doesn't speak German.
But she is confident in her ability to communicate and
navigate whatever comes her way.

I believe that a lifetime of family travel to Europe,
Asia, South America, and most of the United States,
with all kinds of activities, has prepared Kayla to
handle whatever life has in store for her. And I was
lucky enough to get to share many of those enriching
experiences, while building bonds and bridges that will
connect us even when she is all grown up.**"**

Sandra Foyt, founder of Albany Kid
(albanykid.com)

Traveling Like a Local

Once the drive or flight is over and you have finally arrived at your hotel or
vacation rental, it's time to explore. For me, a singular pleasure of travel is
to imagine you live in the place you are visiting. Even though I may have no
intention of ever moving there, I still love the exercise of pretending I have
an apartment in London, or a ski house near Lake Tahoe, or a cottage on the
beach in the Outer Banks.

Children like to keep many of the same routines they have at home, and don't necessarily expect or want their lives to be utterly different when they are on the road. If playing at the park is their favorite thing to do in your neighborhood, it's what they are going to want to do on the road as well. If they nap every afternoon at two o'clock, they are likely to want to do the same while you are traveling. So it is that when you are on the road with kids you can easily enter into the everyday rhythm of a place you are visiting.

How you do this will vary according to the place, of course, but there are a few ways to sample some genuine local flavor while on the road.

Shop and eat local. One of the best ways to get the feel of a new place is to visit local markets or corner restaurants. Are there posters in the entryway of the small, independently owned coffee shop? Stop to read them and see what concerts are being hosted on the library lawn, or when the Rotary Club is having its chicken supper. The fruits and vegetables in the farmers' market will tell you what's growing in the region you are visiting. Even the supermarket will reveal something about the place you are visiting and how the people who live there shop; maybe you'll discover a cooler dedicated to local cheese or an entire shelf full of hot sauce.

Use public transportation. When we stayed in London for a month, I spent my evenings studying the local bus routes until I knew them well enough to be able to hop on and off in different parts of the city.

Tommy was a toddler and loved riding on the top deck of the double-decker buses. Although this wasn't always a convenient way to get around, it meant I got to know the street plan and the neighborhoods, to understand at which point Stoke Newington (our home base) became Islington, and then Finsbury, and then Holborn. As these neighborhoods represent entirely different faces of the city, from 17th-century row houses to Georgian townhouses to postwar apartment blocks, each trip could feel like a journey through culture and history, giving me an understanding of the city I would not otherwise have had.

Tommy loves finding our routes on subway maps.

Maybe it was those early excursions that piqued Tommy's interest, but to this day he likes nothing better than reading a subway map and figuring out how to get where we need to go in a new city.

Find the nearest playground. Once you're there, let your kids loose, and see if you can chat with the other parents. Often they are the best source of tips for what to do with young children in the neighborhood.

Involving ourselves in a community we visit feels natural to my entire family because we've done it so often. Sometimes we wander into the local library. Other times we check out the neighborhood church.

We've rented the same apartment in Paris twice, and we all know where the best bakery is, what days the market is set up on the square, how long it takes us to walk to the Jardin du Luxembourg, and which market stall sells the best rabbit sausage. We may not be Parisians, but for a few days on each visit it feels like we could be. I love that sense of possibility.

Finding a playground, like this one in the Jardin du Luxembourg, Paris, is a great way for kids to have fun and for you to meet some local parents.

Eating on the Road

Other than flying with kids, dining out may be the biggest source of stress for parents planning a trip. Some children are picky eaters and others don't like to sit still, but if you don't provide nourishment on a routine basis, things are unlikely to go well.

Even dining with children who don't yet eat solid food can be problematic. When we decided to take Tommy on the road at the age of three months, we didn't worry too much about how we'd get our dinners. He was a small baby and could sleep in his car seat carrier while we ate. Unfortunately for us, our departure coincided with his decision to start crying every night right at dinnertime.

For almost the entire duration of our trip, Matt and I were unable to have a conversation during a meal because one of us was walking around in the parking lot rocking Tommy while the other one ate.

Although babies and toddlers provide their own set of dining-out challenges (I discuss some of these in the 'Ages and Stages' chapter), there are a few things you can do before you leave home to get ready for on-the-road eating.

When you create your itinerary, scope out your food options. Look for family-friendly restaurants, local farmers' markets, supermarkets, and cafés with outdoor seating that are near the different activities you will be participating in. Many restaurants now share their menus online, making it much easier to determine whether or not your family will enjoy eating there. You'll never go wrong planning to have a meal at a market with many food vendors – everyone can choose to eat what they like, and everyone will be happy.

Eat out occasionally when you are at home. A big part of dining out successfully with kids involves their behavior. If your child never goes to restaurants, then it's not reasonable to expect that he or she will know how to behave in one. Giving your child some training will help them understand expectations when you dine out on the road. As my children have got older, I have increased these expectations beyond simply sitting at the table for a meal, to looking at a menu with a discerning eye and politely ordering their food for themselves – valuable life skills they will use in adulthood.

In Rome, Tommy ate pasta outside, just like the Italians.

Always have snacks handy. Kids have smaller stomachs and greater caloric needs than adults and, therefore, need to eat more often. There have been moments on the road when snacks have unexpectedly had to serve as a meal, so it pays to have a generous assortment.

We stopped on a road trip to eat at this seafood stand, which I had learned online served the best fried clams in Mystic, Connecticut.

Plan to picnic. Picnics provide the greatest flexibility for traveling families. Even if you are staying in a hotel where all you have is a small refrigerator, you can pick up the fixings for a great picnic. If you think you'll be picnicking often, be sure to include a few cold packs in your luggage.

Choose one meal a day to eat in a sit-down restaurant. Make it the one when your child will be best behaved, based on his or her age and schedule. This may mean you eat all of your breakfasts out and have a series of picnic dinners in your hotel room. In countries where restaurants start serving dinner no earlier than seven o'clock, the local culture may make this determination for you – or you may make lunch your big meal of the day.

Don't be afraid to ask a restaurant to help accommodate your child's needs or preferences – if you know that he or she will do best with the sauce on the side, ask for it on the side. Need to get your child's food pronto to avoid a meltdown? Say so! The restaurant staff wants your child to be happy and well behaved as much as you do.

Don't underestimate what your child is willing to eat. One of the best ways to learn about a culture is to sample its food. But that can be tricky when you're traveling with a picky eater who prefers to eat only things that are familiar.

My rule, repeated so often that my children would probably roll their eyes to know that I'm putting it in this book, is "you taste with your mouth, not with your eyes." I never force my kids to eat things they don't like, but they have to try everything at least once. This is how I've ended up with children who love sushi and miso soup, to say nothing of duck, escargot, and lamb chops.

As with all things related to kids and travel, perhaps the most important tip is to be flexible. I let my children bring books to dinner and read them while we're waiting for our food, and sometimes I hand them my phone and let them play a game.

Asian noodle shops are a good bet when eating out with kids; the food comes quickly and is freshly prepared.

Sometimes children just can't handle another meal in a restaurant. Not every meal needs to be a grand cultural experiment, or even tremendously nutritious. It's okay to occasionally eat cereal for dinner.

Making the Most of Museums and Cultural Attractions

We take very few trips that don't involve at least one museum. Even when we are staying at a resort or going far out into the country, we tend to seek out local historical societies and libraries. I am married to a fellow museum-goer so it has always felt natural to visit museums with our kids who, for the most part, share our enthusiasm.

While it's not great that many museums and cultural institutions are struggling to keep up their attendance numbers, the fact that they are struggling is a boon for families. Even small museums now realize how important it is to engage children in their exhibits, and they strive to offer interesting experiences for their youngest visitors. When you arrive at a museum or historic site, make sure to ask if they have any programs or self-guided activities for families.

Here are tips for making the most of your museum visit.

Do your research in advance. Before you visit a museum, take a look at the website to see what's of interest to you and your kids. It's okay if serendipity leads you into some parts of the museum you never expected to visit, but by having a plan you can make sure that you maximize your time. You can also use this as an opportunity to brush up on some facts about the museum's focus that you can share with your children. If you're visiting a historic site, it's also a good idea to familiarize yourself and your children with the history of the place in advance.

Another reason to do a little research is that you may find a given museum has activities available that your children will enjoy. We found that the tourism board of Saint-Emilion, France, had really fun scavenger hunts in English, that Windsor Castle had an audio guide just for children, and that in Williamsburg, we could rent a colonial costume for Teddy that made his experience richer and more interactive.

Don't feel that you have to see the whole thing. It's great to have an ambitious agenda when you visit a museum, especially a large one that's far from your home and holds many classic works of art or historical exhibits you think you 'ought' to see. But you're better off choosing a limited portion of the museum to visit, especially when you are there with children who won't enjoy running from one exhibit to the next just because they are 'supposed to' really see them.

The Oxford Museum of Natural History, in England, offers a scavenger hunt that my children loved completing.

I usually plan to limit museum visits to two to three hours. It's great if the visit lasts longer, but being realistic is one way to make sure your kids stay engaged.

Make connections and ask questions. Take time to read the panels aloud. Talk about what is familiar or unusual in the art or objects you are exploring, and ask open-ended questions designed to get your kids talking about what they see.

Have a scavenger hunt or play 'I-Spy'. Younger children love to look for hidden treasures in museums. This can be a fun way to get them to notice smaller details in artistic work, to find the horn on a dinosaur skeleton, or to see where the steering wheel is in an antique car.

Share opinions. A great way to engage children with art, in particular, is to ask them what they think of it. You might even turn this into a game like this one developed by the staff at the Delaware Art Museum: Give everyone in your family four cards – one with a heart, one with a dollar sign, one with a house, and one that says 'yuck'. Find a room that's not too crowded and ask each person to put a card in front of the work of art that he or she loves the most, likes the least, would take home, and would buy. Once everyone has placed their cards, each person can explain the choices he or she made.

Take advantage of family programs. From story time to guided tours to hands-on activities, many museums offer a huge range of opportunities to get beyond simply looking at the exhibits. Check the website in advance and plan your visit accordingly.

Take a tour. Touring with a guide is an excellent way to meaningfully engage kids in a museum, historic attraction, or city. Amie O'Shaughnessy, founder and publisher of Ciao Bambino! recommends following these best practices when choosing tours for your family:

- Limit tours to three to four hours.
- Work with companies that offer dedicated family itineraries.

- Independent guides are a great option. If you don't have a referral from a reputable source, ask the guide to provide a reference or two from a family that has used their service.
- Typical pricing is $50 or more per hour for a private guide. Group guides may cost less, but you will lose the ability to customize the experience for specific ages and needs.
- On a multi-day trip, using the same guide for different excursions helps ensure continuity and that information will not be repeated.
- Build a treat stop into the tour if possible. Ice cream works wonders to keep everyone motivated and chipper.

Remember that you can leave if a museum or historical site isn't grabbing your kids' attention. They may not be in the mood for it that day – or the museum may just not be that interesting.

Our family-friendly tour of an exhibit at the Philadelphia Museum of Art was engaging and fun – both boys loved answering the guide's questions.

"My mantra is "think creatively and see adventure
and opportunity not roadblocks and hurdles." When
I was six months pregnant with our second daughter,
and my older daughter was only a year old, an
opportunity came up to travel in South Africa. It was
tempting to pass the trip up, but instead we decided
to go and take along my husband's 19-year-old niece.
She was happy to get paid in travel and I was thrilled
to have an extra hand.**"**

Nicole Feliciano, founder of MomTrends
(momtrends.com)

Getting Outdoors

Many parents feel they don't know where to start when it comes to getting outdoors with children. The answer is to start at the beginning. When your children are babies, buy a backpack carrier and go for nature walks or hikes with them. Or invest in a bike trailer or child seat so your child can ride with you.

State and national parks are often set up for inexperienced outdoors people, with abundant information on scenic, interesting hikes or rides of all lengths and levels of difficulty, and trails that are well marked. You can also go on guided trips or take lessons with experts.

Once your child can walk well, the options are pretty much limitless when it comes to outdoor fun. Children as young as two or three years of age can start learning to downhill ski. I had Teddy on a tandem bicycle with me when he was four. Any child who can walk can hike. And the earlier you get your child enrolled in swimming lessons, the earlier it will be safe to get him or her out in a canoe or kayak.

Engage your child with nature. Nature has played a role in most of my family vacations. Even when we visit a city, we almost always spend a lot of time in parks and botanical gardens, riding bikes, or going on urban hikes along old rail trails. We love national parks, wildlife preserves, and any opportunity that brings us into direct contact with flora or fauna. Children almost universally like to be outdoors and whether you like to kayak, bike, canoe, or ski, you're sure to find that your kids will be eager companions.

Even very young children can enjoy the outdoors. Here Tommy, three years old, kayaks with his grandfather.

A great way to get your children interested in being outside is to learn about the ecology of the places you visit – local nature centers, wildlife preserves, or natural history museums often offer guided walks with naturalists. You can also incorporate nature into your trip planning, says Debi Huang, publisher of the blog Go Explore Nature.

"Before you head out on your next trip, find out what's happening in nature at your destination," she says. "Are wildflowers in bloom? Is there seasonal fruit picking? Are there any unique wildlife viewing opportunities?"

Huang also suggests keeping an eye out your window. "When we travel by car, we find ways to connect with nature while we drive," she says. "We watch for wildlife, do some cloud watching, look for new-to-us flowers and trees, or even play our own 'nature bingo' game (this is like traditional car bingo, but we use items from nature instead of road signs and license plates)."

Hiking with kids. From short day hikes to multi-day camping excursions, hiking is one of the simplest ways to get outside with kids. We often have low expectations when it comes to children's physical endurance, but they can go farther and do more than you think they can, even at a young age. Michael Lanza, author of *Before They're Gone: A Family's Year-Long Quest to Explore America's Most Endangered National Parks*, and publisher of The Big Outside, has these tips for making sure your outdoor adventure is a success:

- Bring along motivators for young kids, such as their favorite candy bar to eat halfway through a hike, or a stuffed animal.
- Encourage kids to voice their concerns or tell you when something's bothering them, but establish a rule up front: no whining. Create a dynamic in which a child understands you care and will listen, but that complaining will get him or her nowhere. Everyone will be happier.
- A visibly tired kid is often just a hungry kid. They don't have nearly the fat reserves and muscle mass that adults have, so they need to rest and refuel with food and water much more frequently than adults, sometimes every hour. Look for signs of their gas tank running low: grumpiness, a slowing pace, growing quiet, or a faraway look. Remind them frequently to take

a drink. You'll be surprised how often you see 180-degrees of change in energy level after just a ten-minute rest and a chocolate bar.

• Use positive reinforcement: compliment them when they do well, encourage them when they're challenged. Tell your kids they're good hikers and they will take pride in that.

Some of the most thrilling and satisfying moments I've ever experienced while traveling with my children have been when we've spent time outdoors. I'll never forget how proud Teddy was, when, at three-years-old, he hiked a mile up the Long Trail, in Vermont, to an impressive overlook called Sunset Rock.

On a visit to Chincoteague, Virginia, we saw wild ponies, dug for clams and caught crabs in traps.

Manatee Magic

On a kayak trail in Fort Myers, Florida, a large gray mound rose up right next to the tandem kayak Tommy and I were paddling. It disappeared for just a moment, reappearing on the other side of our boat. I could feel the bulk of the animal's body pressing against us, not in a threatening way, but as if it were nudging us along.

Matt and Teddy paddled over in time to see the face of an enormous manatee as it stuck its nose up to push our kayak with its head. Our kayak moved forward as gently as if a breeze had pushed us. My heart raced. Tommy reached down and put his hand on the animal's back. It dove under our kayak again, teasingly. In that suspended moment there was nothing but dark green water, the blue sky, the four of us, and this animal, reaching out across the boundary of language and environment to say hello.

When Things Don't Go as Planned

We have spent a lot of time exploring all the ways you can help make sure that your family trip is a fun and positive experience for everyone. But, of course, part of the nature of travel – part of the very reason to ever go anywhere – is that things will happen that you didn't anticipate. And while sometimes these things can be happy, like the discovery of a beautiful beach or a great restaurant, at other times they will offer challenges to your entire family.

Whether you are sitting in an airport because your flight has been delayed or have arrived at a museum to find it opens an hour later than you expected, it's important to try to deal with unexpected bumps cheerfully. Remember you are modeling for your kids that travel is fun, and that one aspect of travel is handling unexpected problems.

I thought a tour of the United States Capitol Building would be fun. Teddy, not so much.

Allow your children to be disappointed when something doesn't live up to what they wanted it to, to have days on the trip when they are grumpy, bickering, or say they want to go home, and to fail to be interested in or enjoy something that you really like or were looking forward to.

Forgive yourself for making mistakes as well. I once led my family on a wild goose chase through the Dordogne region of France that resulted in a terribly long drive to visit a disappointingly boring castle. To make matters worse, we were insufficiently provisioned and arrived back in Bordeaux well past dinnertime to discover that the local supermarket had closed. To say my family was annoyed with me would be an understatement. But we got up the next morning and had a fantastic day.

Perhaps the most valuable thing you can learn about traveling with kids is that you shouldn't be afraid to take a day off in the middle of a trip. Sometimes everyone just needs to hang out, get some laundry done, and maybe even watch a bit of television. The last time I checked, there were no family travel police to write you a ticket for catching your breath.

SPECIAL
CONSIDERATIONS
IN FAMILY
TRAVEL

A Memorable Family Travel Pickle

It was ten o'clock and the only movement was a state police car creeping along the shoulder past a seemingly endless line of cars and trucks. The bullhorn stuck out the window was supposed to be telling us what was going on, but the voice that emerged, loud though it was, was unintelligible. I prayed silently that it wouldn't wake up the boys who were both fast asleep in the back seat of our car.

Until we reached this crowded stretch of highway, our trip had been as smooth as glass. As planned, we had picked up the boys right after school and hit the road. I had snacks, dinner, and plenty of activities all ready right in the car.

Our goal was to reach Corolla, North Carolina—the northernmost part of the Outer Banks—by 9:30 p.m. To do so, we had driven south through the entire state of Delaware, into Maryland, and finally onto this tiny and desolate spit of Virginia where the Chesapeake Bay Bridge-Tunnel would carry us across 20 miles of water to Norfolk.

Then, with no warning whatsoever, traffic came to a complete halt. We sat in the middle of numerous idling trucks, trying to ignore the fumes, and watching as ominous clouds rolled across the sky. After about 20 minutes, I pulled out our tablet and learned that the approaching storm and its high winds had caused a truck to tip over on the bridge. Until they could clear it, which they couldn't do until the storm passed and the winds died down, no traffic would be allowed to pass.

We started out, as one always does, cheerful and resolute. We told stories and read as the light faded. When the storm really hit, we had to roll up the windows to avoid getting soaked and the air in the car quickly turned soupy.

Bickering began as we tried to decide what was worse: being stuffy and hot or being wet. An hour passed. Two hours. Finally the boys fell asleep. With nothing else to do, Matt and I did as well, waking when the state police car arrived with its garbled explanation or when an especially strong gust of wind hit the car.

At one o'clock in the morning the state trooper returned for a slow parade with his bullhorn, clearly doing his best to make sure everyone woke up. It took another 25 minutes for traffic to start moving, and when it did, we realized just how close we were to the toll booths, probably about a mile from where we had been sitting.

Once we got onto the bridge, the rest of the traffic seemed to disappear, perhaps into the seething water below us, as we drove on the surreal bridge to nowhere. Descending into the illuminated glare of the tunnel halfway across did nothing to jar us back to reality and we rode like sleepwalkers until, just as we reached the opposite shore, we saw the truck that had caused all the trouble. It looked as if it had been cast aside by a petulant child and then stepped on, its trailer dented and torn.

I stayed awake with Matt for the remaining two hours of the drive. When we arrived at our condo, the boys, alert after their few hours of sleep, started to bounce off the walls of their room. Before things got too out of hand, Matt said some choice things in a loud voice. (Who am I to judge? I was so tired that I put sunscreen on my toothbrush). Inspired by fear, the kids fell asleep immediately, as did we – the blissful, dark sleep that only comes at the point of total exhaustion. The last thing I remember was glancing at the clock, which showed four o'clock in the morning.

Despite this, the weekend ended up being just fine – better than fine, actually. The next morning we all played putt-putt golf, and the boys rode in go-karts. In the brisk air of the Currituck Sound our long stay at the bridge seemed only a bad dream.

And now we have a story, one that can grow and become more elaborate over time. I'm sure that by the time Tommy and Teddy share it with their children, we'll have been sitting on that highway for 12 hours and lightning will have struck our car. I'll never forget that silent drive across the bridge when I watched my husband in profile and caught glimpses of the roiling water beneath us. We were allies in that moment, fellow travelers on an adventure.

Bad weather on our trip to North Carolina meant the no 'swimming' flag was up for the duration of our trip. Tommy wasn't as disappointed as he looks here – it was cold!

Thinking Safety Before You Go

The amount of time you spend thinking about safety before your trip will vary with your kids' ages, needs, and also the destinations you'll be visiting – obviously you don't need to worry as much about a road trip to Grandma's house as a journey to the developing world. Let's take a look at some things you can do to make travel with kids safe – before leaving home.

Safety Questions You Need Answered

Here are some questions you'll want to address:

- **Is your child up-to-date on all of his or her vaccines? If you'll be traveling to a country in the developing world, will he or she need any special vaccines or preventative medicine?** Your child's pediatrician should be able to answer both of these questions for you. The CDC Traveler's Health website also has information about this for individual countries; when you search, check the box that says you are traveling with children.
- **Is the water safe to drink where you will be traveling?** The CDC site can also advise you about water safety; if it is a concern you may want to invest in a portable water purification system like those offered by SteriPEN before you leave home. You can also purchase bottled water while on the road.
- **What does your health insurance cover while on the road?** A call to your insurance company can clarify the costs of taking your child to an emergency clinic or hospital while you are on the road. My children have had ailments ranging from a broken arm to an appendicitis scare to painful swimmer's ear while traveling, and it has always been good to know where I should seek treatment and how much it would cost.
- **Should you buy travel insurance?** Yes, especially if your trip is expensive, or involves travel to remote destinations where it would be hard to get home in an emergency situation. For different costs, you can have different levels of coverage, including medical evacuation.

A public fountain in Rome. Tommy and I chose only to play in it, not to drink from it.

What to pack. You'll also want to be prepared for anything that might happen while you're traveling. Here is a list of what to put in your bag:

- *Emergency contacts.* Make a series of index cards or business cards for each piece of baggage, your children's backpacks, and your own wallets that list the following: your child's name, your name and, if you have a spouse or partner, his or her name and cell phone number, the local address where you are staying, two additional emergency contact names and phone numbers, your child's pediatrician's name and phone number, and your insurance information.

Your child should have identifying information like this with him or her at all times on your trip – you can fold it up and put it in a pocket. It's also a good idea for you to keep a more detailed master list of all emergency contacts and your child's vaccinations and prescriptions with you while traveling. Here you can include contact information for your child's ophthalmologist, dentist, and any other specialist he or she sees. If you will be traveling out of the country, include contact information for the nearest embassy or consulate.

- *Maps.* Part of staying safe is knowing where you are. You need a paper backup in case your GPS or cell phone won't work or you run out of power.
- *A first aid kit.* Include bandages, antiseptic wipes, children's pain relief, tweezers, and instant ice packs.
- *Prescription medications.* Have these in sufficient quantities to last for the duration of your trip and a bit beyond. Carry a paper copy of the prescription as well.
- *Spare pairs of glasses.* Children who wear glasses should always have a spare pair; it's a good idea to pack his or her eyeglass prescription as well.
- *The emergency number for each country you'll visit.* Be sure to look this up before you hit the road. The United States State Department maintains a list of emergency numbers around the world.

Safety on the Road

Whether you are taking a two-hour road trip to your family's cabin, or flying halfway around the world, traveling with kids offers challenges that other types of travel do not. Keeping kids safe and healthy on the road and making the trip fun for them (and you) at different ages requires both planning and some extra effort.

Airplane safety. Although the Federal Aviation Administration (FAA) allows children under two to be held in their parents' laps, I never felt especially safe doing this and started buying my children plane tickets when they were babies. Doing so also gave us some much needed extra space, and often my children would sleep in their car seats on the plane.

This is a personal decision, and since very few people are injured or die fro. airplane turbulence each year, you may quite reasonably make the choice to hold your child in your lap. This will certainly save you money, and some children prefer it.

If your child will be traveling on your lap, you need to bring his or her birth certificate with you to the airport as proof of age. In addition, some airlines require that you have tickets for lap children. Check in advance of your trip.

The American Academy of Pediatrics and the FAA recommend using a car safety seat with a label indicating that it is FAA approved until your child weighs 40 pounds and can safely sit in the airplane seat with the belt buckled[3]. Bring your car seat manual with you on the plane so you can refer to it if you have questions about how best to install it, and can show the pictures to a flight attendant to prove you've positioned it properly.

You are not allowed to use belt-positioning booster seats on airplanes, but the FAA has approved use of the CARES system for children weighing between 22 and 44 pounds[4]. This is a lighter weight harness that restrains your child's shoulders in an airline seat. CARES is only for use on airplanes, but if you won't need a car seat once you get to your destination, it's a good solution because it's much less bulky and easier to pack and carry.

Car seat safety. It is a pain to haul car seats on trips because they are bulky and heavy. Although car seats do not count against your baggage allowance on most airlines, I would never check my child's car seat for two reasons: I'm not confident that it would be gently handled, and I would worry that it might get lost. On domestic flights in the United States you can usually check your child's car or booster seat at the gate for no additional cost if you don't want to use it on the plane.

Renting car seats at your destination is an option, but it's also a case of buyer beware, as you can't be certain what condition available car seats will be in. Alternatives to renting a car seat include borrowing one from a trusted friend, or purchasing a new one at your destination. Another option is to plan your

.rip so you won't need car seats – if you use only public transportation, it won't be an issue.

In many parts of the world, taxis don't have seatbelts, and car seats are not readily available. Renting your own car from a reputable agency or paying for a family-friendly driver or tour can be the best way to make sure you have proper restraints. Be sure to research what's available before you travel and determine your own comfort level with the vehicle restraints available to you.

Hotel room safety. The best way to keep little ones safe in your hotel or vacation rental is by keeping an eye on them. There are a few simple things you can do to create a safer environment in the places you stay.

- Move anything breakable or heavy off surfaces where little hands can grab it, and put trash cans out of reach.
- Travel with plastic outlet covers. They are small, light, and easy to stick in your luggage. You might also bring some painter's tape to cover outlets. This can also come in handy to tape over any sharp edges on the furniture, and to tape dresser drawers shut.
- My kids always slept in cribs, so on the road we borrowed them from hotels. Double check to make sure the crib is sturdy once you've set it up, and check the bedding is secure. Even if your child usually sleeps with you, a crib can be a handy form of containment for a few moments, so you may want to request one. The crib should be placed away from the drapes or anything else that your child could possibly grab.
- When you run a bath, make sure the water isn't scalding. Hotel water can be hot, so it's a good idea to check the water temperature, even with older kids who normally bathe themselves.
- Check to make sure windows and doors close and lock securely.

Never leave young children alone in a hotel room or vacation rental. Teens can safely be left only if you both have working cell phones.

Crowd safety. One of my biggest fears on the crowded, hectic London Underground was losing my children. Babies and young children can go in carriers and strollers, but my kids both stopped wanting to be in a stroller by the time they were about four-years-old.

My policy has been to rely on good, old-fashioned vigilance and lots of hand-holding when we are in crowded situations, but I also make sure my children have the index cards I described earlier on their person and in their backpack should they be wearing one.

As soon as my kids were old enough to understand the concept of an adult in uniform, I took time before and during our trips to talk to them about what they should do if they got lost in a crowd: find an adult dressed as a security guard or police officer, explain what has happened, and share the index card. In cases where they don't speak the language, they should simply show the person the card. I also point out adults in uniform when I see them and remind my kids that those are the people they can always ask for help.

A pleasure of traveling is getting to know strangers and sometimes relying on their kindness. But it is not prudent to leave your children alone with strangers while traveling, unless they are pre-screened babysitters or nannies. (I talk about childcare in the 'Finding Adult Time on the Road' chapter.)

Water safety. There are two kinds of water safety to be aware of when traveling: consumption and immersion. You can safely drink water from the tap in most of the developed world. In countries where the water isn't safe because of the danger of waterborne illness, you should avoid consuming it under any condition. That means brushing your teeth with treated water, and avoiding ice cubes in your beverages.

As far as swimming is concerned, the easiest way to keep your child safe in the water is to supervise at all times. Keep young children within reach in the water. Make sure someone is watching older children who know how to swim.

Practice safety in and around pools. Children shouldn't run poolside and they shouldn't dive into water that is less than nine feet deep. Children should never swim near or touch pool drains, and before you go in the water, make sure drain covers aren't loose because they can create dangerous suction.

Food safety. Practice common sense food safety measures on the road with children. In countries where the water isn't safe, avoid raw produce that has likely been washed in it, unless it has a peel you can remove.

If you are planning to eat a lot of picnics on the road, invest in a thermal bag or backpack and a cold pack to help keep food fresh.

Make sure your children wash their hands with soap before eating. A pack of antibacterial wipes will work in a pinch, and can also be used to clean off any utensils that look like they haven't been sterilized.

Jodi Ettenberg, founder of the blog Legal Nomads and author of *The Food Traveler's Handbook*, offers these tips on food safety when traveling with kids in the developing world:

- Be sure to completely peel fruit.
- Try street food – choose a vendor where you can see that the preparation and cooking process is clean, and they are not touching money and then touching the food. Lines where there are women and children waiting for food are a good bet, and an addition to the 'go with the crowds' adage for street food.
- For longer train rides and bus rides, bags of oranges are a great snack and an icebreaker to offer up to other families with their kids.
- Bring portable chopsticks when experimenting with food. They make eating more fun for kids (since you need to screw them together and then use them thereafter, it's a magic utensil on-the-go) and they are great for when street food itself is clean and fresh but the utensils look questionable.
- Visit dawn markets. They're an ideal way to learn about the way a country eats, shops, and handles its own produce. They are also a fabulously chaotic and colorful introduction to a new place.

If your child has food allergies, you will need to be more careful about what ~~he~~ or she eats on the road and will likely need to bring and prepare more of your own food while traveling.

Sun and heat safety. You probably practice sun and heat safety at home, but on the road it can be a little bit trickier as you may be in less controlled environments, and out exploring more. If you are visiting a destination with a climate that is very hot, it's wise to avoid being outside in the middle of the day when the heat and sun are at their most intense.

There are three easy things you need to remember about keeping your child safe in the heat: provide plenty of drinks (ideally one every 15 minutes, even when your child is swimming), make sure that you apply sunscreen regularly, and keep your child well fed with lots of hydrating snacks such as fruits and cut vegetables.

It is also important to be savvy about sun exposure. Practice age-appropriate sun protection. Keep very young babies out of direct sunlight, and in the shade. For older babies and toddlers, use a barrier sunscreen that contains zinc oxide or titanium dioxide (or both). Older children should wear a broad-spectrum sunscreen with an SPF of 30 or greater, and which protects against both UVA and UVB rays[5].

And don't skimp on the sunscreen either – a full ounce is what it takes to cover most kids' exposed skin. Feel the need to measure it? Grab a shot glass.

You can't beat sun-protective clothing, sunglasses and hats to keep kids' skin and eyes safe. If you will be visiting a location where it's tricky to stock up on sunblock, you might consider this as a good alternative.

Safety in the cold. Make sure your children are dressed appropriately in dry layers (a reason I favor staying in accommodations with a dryer when on family ski trips). Encourage them to go inside routinely to warm up and have some hot chocolate, especially when the temperature is below freezing.

afety in the woods. If you are camping or spending time outside where ticks are a problem (the Centers for Disease Control has some excellent maps and explanations showing this information[6]) you can protect your child with bug spray containing 10 percent DEET on exposed areas, paying special attention to the skin on your child's neck or directly above his or her socks. If you prefer to avoid DEET, look for bug spray containing picaridin, which has a more environmentally friendly reputation, but also protects from harmful bites.

Helmets and bug spray = mountain biking safety.

If you are spending time on your trip hiking or camping, get in the habit of doing a tick check as part of your nighttime routine. Look behind ears, knees, and elbows, and check your child's trunk and neck as well.

Use tweezers to remove any ticks you find and save them in a bag to show your doctor. Keep an eye out for the telltale bull's-eye that indicates your child has Lyme disease, or for symptoms like a fever, abdominal pain, or muscle pain, which can indicate Rocky Mountain Spotted Fever. Call your doctor right away if your child experiences any of these symptoms.

If your child has asthma or allergies and may need a nebulizer while you are camping, make sure you have one that operates on batteries or have access to electricity as needed. Don't rely on your cell phone to work in remote areas and always have a battery-operated radio with you.

When Your Child Gets Sick or Injured on the Road

It's never fun when your child suffers, and being far away from home can make even minor issues seem worse. If you travel often with kids, some sickness or injury is inevitable, just as it is at home. But illness or injury doesn't have to ruin your trip.

Common problems to look out for. Motion sickness may be the most common problem children experience on the road. Sitting in the forward-facing seat, looking out the window, stopping for fresh air, or sucking on a lollipop can all help. Your child's doctor may also recommend medication if his or her motion sickness is more severe.

Changes in cabin pressure during takeoff and landing in an airplane can be painful if your child is at all congested. Nursing or sucking on a pacifier can help babies and young children; older children can chew gum or suck on a lollipop.

Diarrhea is a very common travel problem for people of all ages. Keeping children hydrated is important – if possible, find some electrolyte solution.

Altitude sickness is another common tricky issue, because it can hit without warning, even if your child has never suffered it before. The symptoms also vary from nausea to jitters. Give your family time to acclimate. And make sure your child drinks extra fluids, as dehydration can make the symptoms of altitude sickness worse.

Managing minor problems. If you suspect your child isn't feeling well while you are on the road, act quickly. Don't wait to start pushing fluids, extra rest, or pain reliever.

Notice a rash or something else that's not right? Contact your child's pediatrician, even if you're abroad. Often a phone call to the doctor can help you get ahead of whatever your child is suffering from, and if he or she needs any kind of prescription, you'll be able to get it more readily.

Even if you're in a country where pharmacists can help diagnose and dispense medicine that requires a prescription in the United States, having your doctor's recommendation about what to give your child will give you a starting point for any conversation, which is especially handy when there is a language barrier.

If your child gets sick or hurt, it's best to accept it and adjust your plans and expectations accordingly. Taking a day off from your itinerary and spending it in your hotel room resting is a much better idea than muscling along like nothing is wrong.

Finding a doctor on the road. In the United States, many towns and cities now offer urgent care clinics where you can seek emergency care for your child at all hours of the day or night without going to the hospital. Even when you travel abroad, emergency care is often just a phone call away.

When Tommy was a toddler and we were spending a month in London, the extremely hot coffee in my cup sloshed through the safety lid and onto his neck as he sat in his stroller. His screams were immediate, penetrating, and terrifying for me, and I did the only thing I could think to do, which was call 999 (the UK emergency number).

An ambulance came to our door, and Tommy and I were taken to the nearest pediatric emergency room, where the doctor prescribed paraffin oil and pain relief, and sent us home after making a follow-up appointment. Although I offered my insurance card, we were not charged for the ride or the treatment.

In many places you travel with your children, you will be able to seek emergency help without a second thought. But if that is not possible – because you are in a remote area or a country without extensive developed medical care – you should rely on your country's embassy or consulate to help you find a doctor who speaks English. For more information about how to find a doctor abroad, see the United States State Department's website[7].

"My husband and I both work full-time and our son spends most of his time at day care or sleeping. When we travel, we get to spend every minute with him. We're thankful to have these moments together, and know that he will grow up far too fast. So it's important that we introduce him to the world now. Every travel experience is teaching him new things about himself and the world around him, and it's also teaching us in the process.**"**

Nicole Wears, founder, with her husband Cam,
of The Traveling Canucks (travelingcanucks.com)

Ages and Stages

It would be easy to dedicate an entire book to traveling with kids at each stage of development because each of them requires something different. For detailed information and tips, you'll find age-specific websites and books in the 'Resources' section at the end of this book. But let's take a quick look at some of the special considerations for kids of different ages.

Tommy catching a nap on the go in Venice Beach, California.

Travel with babies. Perhaps the easiest children to travel with: babies' needs are simple and straightforward, they don't voice their opinions about what to do, and they can sleep and eat anywhere.

If you are breastfeeding your baby, you can nurse when you need to, although having a scarf as a cover-up is a good idea. Formula is available all over the world, although if it's important to you that your child eats a specific bran you may want to bring enough with you to cover your baby's needs on the trip. You can also have formula shipped to you while you are on the road.

Diapers are sized differently in different countries, and the weight and size on the box will be in metric once you get outside the United States. This means you might want to know how big your child is in kilos and centimeters, not just pounds and inches, so you don't waste money on diapers that are the wrong size.

It can be tempting to bring a ton of gear with you when you have a baby. At home you probably have a lot of specialized equipment. But learning to improvise can actually be part of your travel experience.

" *It can be difficult to find baby-changing tables, high chairs, or stroller-accessibility when traveling (especially outside the United States), but rather than look at it as a frustrating negative, see it as an opportunity to get creative. I learned to change my baby on a closed toilet seat, on top of a sink (put your diaper bag inside to make a flat surface), and in her stroller in public restrooms. People will surprise you with help, too; when encountering a broken elevator, a London Tube employee carried my stroller up the stairs himself, and restaurant managers in Turkey will often offer their own offices for changing and feeding. If you don't expect the world to cater to you, you can be amazed at the kindness of strangers, as well as your own resourcefulness!* **"**

Meg Nesterov, freelance writer and publisher of The Notorious M.E.G. (thenotoriousmeg.com)

---

ravel with toddlers. I spent 13 months traveling with a toddler, and if there's one thing I learned it's that this age is not for the faint of heart. Children between the ages of one and three are mobile and opinionated while lacking basic life-preserving skills.

Many of the same rules of traveling with babies apply to toddlers as well – it's definitely best to be prepared with plenty of diapers, clothing changes, and snacks, not to mention a bag of tricks (board books, small toys) to pull out in a pinch.

Tommy loved riding double-decker buses in London when he was a toddler.

As your child becomes increasingly mobile and learns to walk, you're likely find that a big part of your travel will become a tactile exploration of the world around you. I spent more hours than I can count watching Tommy throw rocks into water – from the fountains of the Boboli Garden in Florence, Italy, to the shores of Town Lake in Austin, Texas.

Children this age love to move and explore with their hands, and the more opportunities you can give them to do this, the happier your journeying together will be. It's a great age to visit parks, zoos, playgrounds, children's museums, or to spend hours at the beach or in the woods.

The most important thing about traveling with a toddler is to have realistic expectations. This is not the ideal age to plan lots of meals at restaurants— your child is unlikely to want to sit through them, and will probably be quite vocal in expressing displeasure.

When you do eat out, choose restaurants that welcome children, those with outdoor seating areas where your child can wander without disrupting other diners, and places where you can get your food relatively quickly.

Make sure your trip itineraries include plenty of time to move, and to take daily naps as needed. And be prepared for the inevitable disruptions of travel to disrupt your child's sleep.

Travel with tweens and teens. Diapers and car seats may be a thing of the past, but that doesn't mean that traveling with older kids is easy. Here are tips for keeping harmony and enjoying these last precious years of family travel.

- **Involve your tween or teen in planning the trip.** From the minute you start planning to go away, talk to your child about where he or she would like to go, and what they would like to do. You might even consider handing over one entire day of your trip to your teen, letting him or her choose everything from the activities to where you will dine.

Mary Turner, publisher of the blog Travel with Teens and Tweens also suggests having teens pack for themselves, but double-checking what they bring; her son once forgot to bring his bathing suit on a beach trip.

- **Give them access to their friends from the road.** Give your tween or teen permission and time to communicate with their friends in ways that are most affordable and make sense given your destination. Traveling domestically? A limited amount of texting might be acceptable, or you might let your child have access to friends through email or social networks.

This is also a great age to invite friends along for the trip if that is possible, or to travel with another family with kids of a similar age.

Teens and tweens enjoy pushing the envelope and being independent.

- **Be realistic about screen time.** You might have visions of an entirely unplugged family vacation, but if the end result is a sulky kid, you're not likely to enjoy yourself much. Turner suggests negotiating clear ground rules before you hit the road. "Whether it's expectations about using electronics or bringing along a friend, it helps to have clear ground rules up front," she says. "We find that stating our goals, but then listening to other options and being willing to compromise can make for a positive experience all around."

- **Do something active that they enjoy.** Getting outdoors and getting active make it hard for anyone to stay in a bad mood. But Turner also recommends knowing when to let your teen relax. "Be flexible about early mornings versus opportunities to sleep in. Our teens are so busy that sometimes just taking a break is the best thing to do on vacation."

- **Let them have some independence.** Whether you let your teen hang out in the hotel game room without you, or sign your tween up for a kids-only day-long kayaking lesson, older kids will relish whatever moments of age-appropriate independence you allow them.

- **Plan for some family time.** A benefit of traveling with your teen is the chance (often rare at home) to spend some uninterrupted time together. Turner suggests taking advantage of this by bringing your favorite family game.

"Some of our favorite memories involve a family game night on the road," she says "It is about the only time we can all settle down together uninterrupted by school, sports or work."

Carol Cain, publisher of the blog Girl Gone Travel, agrees that time together is part of the value of traveling with your teen, and she recommends ignoring sighs and eye rolls.

"Don't assume your teen would rather not be with you when traveling, or that they are bored," she says. "Your teen is listening, and is interested, as long as you remember to listen and remain interested in them too. My teen spends most of the time quiet and stoic during our travel, until, when I least expect it, he shares funny observations. Teens are still very much like sponges and when they are ready they will show you just how much they've learned."

My favorite piece of advice about traveling with teens also comes from Cain: "If your teen asks you to dance with them, do it like no one is watching."

Multi-family or Multi-generational Travel

Traveling with another family, or with multiple generations of your own, can be a meaningful way for you and your children to connect with other adults and children. You'll have the added benefit of having extra sets of hands to help you with your kids and, if you are traveling with a family that also has children, your kids will have companions other than you.

Teddy and his great grandfather on a four-generation family trip.

Planning multi-family travel. Use the same considerations when planning this trip as you do for your own family journeys, but make sure you take everyone into account. There should be activities that every member of the group will enjoy. Remember not everyone has to participate in every activity; it's okay to split up into smaller groups.

Before you go, make clear decisions about who will cover what costs. If you will be preparing food, set a meal schedule so that one person doesn't become the personal chef.

Don't assume that everyone has to stay in the same place – although it can be fun to pile together into one big house, if one family has a baby who cries all night, they might be more comfortable in their own condo or cottage.

Traveling with an elderly person. Dana Freeman, publisher of the website Find and Go Seek, has traveled multiple times with her husband, children, and 90-plus grandmother. She suggests keeping the following things in mind when traveling with an elderly person:

- Make sure your accommodations are either on one level or have an elevator. Cruise ships are a great option.
- Allow extra time for getting to places, and make sure you have access to a wheelchair whenever possible (e.g. for museums or sightseeing).
- Be careful about dehydration and overheating; make sure you have plenty of water with you.
- Recognize the senior may be stubborn and think he or she can do more than is realistic.
- Plan for some downtime with everyone together. Encourage the older person to share stories, and bring a journal so you can capture them to share with future generations.

Finding Adult Time on the Road

No matter what age your children are or who you are traveling with, it's a good idea to find ways to have a little time apart from them either on your own or with your spouse or partner.

If you have working cell phones and are traveling with teens, you may be able to safely leave them in your hotel room or vacation rental. But what about younger kids? Here are some tips on finding childcare on the road:

• Many hotels and resorts offer either a kids club or a vetted nanny service. The concierge will be able to help you with both options. You should feel free to ask to meet anyone who will be providing care for your child beforehand so that you can interview them.

• If you know someone with kids in the destination you are visiting, ask them to recommend a local babysitter. See if you can set up a phone or Skype call before your trip to interview that person.

• If you are traveling overseas, you can also check with study abroad offices for either your alma mater or a local university to see if any students studying there might be interested in babysitting. Again, use Skype to interview prospective sitters in advance.

• Many cities have nanny or childcare agencies that will help you book a babysitter.

• It can pay to bring a babysitter with you. When we went to Paris for the first time we took along the reliable, responsible daughter of family friends who had just graduated from high school. I used airline miles to buy her plane ticket and rented an apartment that was big enough to accommodate all of us. For the cost of her flight, accommodation, and food, we ended up with a delightful companion who watched the boys on numerous nights of our trip.

Tommy threw a coin in the Trevi Fountain in Rome, which means he will one day return.

It is a highly personal decision whether or not to trust a stranger with your child, or whether to leave your child alone. If you aren't comfortable with one-on-one care, you might consider signing your child up for a local day camp or activity.

If that's not an option, stay in accommodations where you can put the children to bed, and eat a nice meal that you have cooked or had delivered in another room. The simple act of having some kid-free quiet time, even if they are snoozing in the next room, can be very rejuvenating.

What Are the Challenges of Family Travel?

It would be disingenuous of me to talk about family travel only in glowing and positive terms. There are times when traveling with kids is tremendously challenging, and when I end up doing things that I don't really enjoy and wouldn't choose to do without them.

Would I have spent an entire day out of a four-day trip to Colonial Williamsburg riding the Lazy River at Water Country USA if I were there on my own? Would I have given over a precious day in Paris to the children's museum there? I'll let you guess the answer to both of those questions. To travel successfully with kids you must compromise.

Traveling with kids isn't always a pure vacation, even if you've planned it as such. Even if you are staying at a luxurious resort or trying to relax on the beach, kids get sick, they refuse to sleep, and sometimes they are fussy and difficult.

When Matt and I left to spend a year on the road with Tommy, he was a year old, and I was as new to the parenting business as I was to traveling with children. It sometimes felt like I had to learn the family travel lessons of compromise and flexibility over and over again.

A Grown-Up Birthday on the Road

The first stop on our trip was Boston, where we spent a difficult month in a disappointing short-term rental apartment, surrounded on all sides by students who partied late into the night. On my 33rd birthday we were two weeks into our stay and decided to go over to Quincy Market and the North End, which is one of the oldest parts of the city and also Boston's Little Italy.

I had spent every minute of my free time during the preceding two weeks reading travel books about Boston. One in particular enchanted me. It described all of the city's ethnic neighborhoods, including lists of where to eat. Because the author was interested in the quirky, these restaurants tended to be hole-in-the-wall places lacking space for a high chair and serving food that most self-respecting toddlers would consign to the floor. She also listed wonderful walking tours full of historical detail.

On my birthday, I wanted the day to be 'nice'. Pre-Tommy nice. No careful packing of cut-up grapes in the backpack. Liquor. Served in breakable glasses. I carried my book of walking tours with me, clutching it to my breast like a street evangelist with a Bible.

When we arrived at Quincy Market, we discovered that the public TV station was sponsoring a jazz and blues festival, which meant incredibly loud, pulsing music and huge crowds of people. Leaving Tommy and Matt to enjoy it, I fought through the masses in the food court in search of Tommy's lunch. Getting thoroughly sweaty and disheveled in the process, I somehow managed to find a stand selling the worst clam chowder in the whole of Boston, which, much to my disgust, Tommy refused to eat. He preferred instead to sit in a puddle, bounce to the music, and munch on oyster crackers.

He had made many friends by the time we left, but I was unwilling to delight in his antics.

As we walked over to the North End, I could feel my unhappiness building: why was I hauling the heavy bag? When was I going to have a chance to look at my book? Matt and I hadn't even discussed where we might have our lunch.

But then I looked at Tommy. We were walking through the Big Dig, the enormous construction zone that at that time separated the North End from the rest of the city. His shorts were muddy and his face was sticky with rejected chowder. Matt exclaimed over the tableau of construction equipment before us and Tommy stared with overwhelming delight, pointing in amazement as if he had never seen a dump truck before.

I quietly put my guidebook in the diaper bag and started to have fun just being with Tommy. Because he hadn't eaten his soup, we soon had to feed him, which we did in the shady mall that borders the Old North Church. Although I'd probably visited five times on previous trips to Boston, I'd always been so focused on getting into the church where Paul Revere hung his lanterns that I never admired his statue or the Italianate fountain in this lovely plaza. It was full of pigeons and locals walking their dogs. Tommy ate grapes and happily pointed at each new animal that passed.

When he was finished, I thought we would move on, but he struggled against the straps on his stroller. I released him, and he carefully made his way around the perimeter of the fountain, using the rim to support himself. Completing his circumnavigation, he toddled unsteadily over to a small gate and stood there, rattling it.

The gate turned out to be the entrance to a peaceful little alcove dedicated to Saint Francis. With a look of utter satisfaction, Tommy slowly maneuvered himself up onto a bench and beamed at us. Somewhere, church bells rang. We all sat and felt the breeze on our skin, watching from our own private garden as the tourists bustled through on the Freedom Trail, intent on reaching the church and entirely missing the quiet spot Tommy had led us to.

As we put Tommy back in his stroller to continue our walk, I saw a young couple sitting on a bench in the main plaza, poring over the same book I had put away. I almost asked them to enjoy a glass of champagne on my behalf, but instead I just smiled at my boy.

The most vital thing to know and remember about traveling with children is the importance of suspending your expectations. I write a family-travel blog. My main goal is to inspire parents to leave the comfort and safety of their homes and share the world with their children, whether that world encompasses their neighborhood, their town, or a different continent.

When we leave our homes, we leave behind the web of possessions and accumulated to-do lists and focus on spending time together. When we travel with our kids, we show them how precious and interesting the world is, and encourage them to think about preserving it and making it better. We don't know what's going to happen tomorrow, but when we look back on years of rich experiences we won't regret a single one. Traveling with kids helps us to become our better selves.

RESOURCES

Planning Family Travel

Planning Itineraries/Choosing a Destination

- Minitime (minitime.com)
- The Perrin Post (cntraveler.com/perrin-post)
- Trekaroo (trekaroo.com)

Transportation

- Hipmunk (hipmunk.com)
- Kayak (kayak.com)
- Department of Transportation Aviation Consumer Protection website (dot.gov/airconsumer)

Lodging

- HomeAway (homeaway.com)
- VRBO (vrbo.com)
- AirBnB (airbnb.com)
- GoWithOh (Europe only) (gowithoh.com)
- Roomerama (roomorama.com)
- FlipKey (flipkey.com)
- CiaoBambino! (ciaobambino.com)

Camping

- Recreation.gov (recreation.gov)
- Go Camping America (gocampingamerica.com)
- RV Park Reviews (rvparkreviews.com)
- RV-camping.org (RV-camping.org)

Cruises

- Family Cruise section of CruiseCritic.com (cruisecritic.com/cruisestyles/area.cfm?area=23)
- Wendy Perrin, 'Before Booking a Family Cruise Ask Yourself These 10 Questions', The Perrin Post, cntraveler.com/perrin-post/2013/03/family-cruise-vacation-tips-questions, 2013
- Suzanne Rowan Kelleher, 'Kid-friendly Cruises: An Age-by-Age Guide to Cruising', Minitime, minitime.com/trip-tips/Kidfriendly-Cruises-article

Games and Apps for Kids
- Best Kids Apps (bestkidsapps.com)
- 'Road Trip Boredom Busters', KidsHealth.org, kidshealth.org/parent/ positive/family/road_trip.html

Apps to Use on the Road
- TripIt (https://tripit.com)
- GateGuru (gateguruapp.com)
- LocalEats (localeats.com/localeats-mobile/)
- Google Maps (google.com/mobile/maps/)
- AroundMe (aroundme.com)
- HopStop (hopstop.com)
- Uber (uber.com)

Cultural Travel with Kids
- Bill Richards and E. Ashley Steel, *Family on the Loose: The Art of Traveling With Kids* (Bellvue, Washington: Rumble Books, 2012)
- The Culture Mom (theculturemom.com)
- This Is My Happiness (thisismyhappiness.com)

Outdoor/Adventure Travel with Kids
- Michael Lanza, *Before They're Gone: A Family's Year-Long Quest to Explore America's Most Endangered National Parks* (Boston: Beacon Press, 2012)
- Pit Stops for Kids (pitstopsforkids.com)
- Go Explore Nature (goexplorenature.com)
- Wandermom (wandermom.com)

Safety
- CDC Traveler's Health website (wwwnc.cdc.gov/travel)
- KidsHealth (kidshealth.org)
- United States State Department, 'Find a Doctor or Hospital Abroad'. travel.state.gov/travel/tips/emergencies/emergencies_1195.html, 2013

- CDC Geographic distribution of ticks (cdc.gov/ticks/geographic_distribution.html)
- Emergency phone numbers around the world (studentsabroad.state.gov/content/pdfs/911_ABROAD.pdf)

Ages and Stages
Traveling With Babies and Toddlers
- Have Baby Will Travel (havebabywilltravel.com)
- Travels with Baby (travelswithbaby.com)
Traveling with Teens and Tweens
- Travel With Teens and Tweens (travel-with-teens.com)
- Girl Gone Travel (girlgonetravel.com)

Other Traveling Families
- Hip Travel Mama (hiptravelmama.com)
- Globetrotting Mama (globetrottingmama.com)
- Walking On Travels (walkingontravels.com)
- Arrows Sent Forth (arrowssentforth.com)
- The Notorious M.E.G. (thenotoriousmeg.com)
- Wandering Pod (wanderingpod.com)
- The Carey Adventures (thecareyadventures.com/blog/)
- Suitcases and Sippycups (suitcasesandsippycups.com)
- The Vacation Gals (thevacationgals.com)
- Family on the Loose (familyontheloose.com)
- Find and Go Seek (indandgoseek.net)
- MomTrends (momtrends.com)
- Traveling Canucks (travelingcanucks.com)
- Albany Kid (albanykid.com)
- Travel Savvy Mom (travelsavvymom.com)
- Almost Fearless (almostfearless.com)

Endnotes

[1]"Fly Rights: A Consumer Guide to Air Travel," Department of Transportation Aviation Consumer Protection, http://www.dot.gov/airconsumer

[2]"Road Trip Boredom Busters," KidsHealth.org, http://kidshealth.org/parent/ firstaid_safe/ outdoor/road_trip.html

[3]"Travel Safety Tips," American Academy of Pediatrics, http://www.aap.org/en-us/about-the-aap/ aap-press-room/news-features-and-safety-tips/pages/Travel-Safety-Tips.aspx

[4]"Child Safety: Keep Your Little Ones Safe When You Fly," Federal Aviation Administration, http://www.faa.gov/passengers/fly_children/

[5]"Sun Safety," KidsHealth.org, http://kidshealth.org/parent/firstaid_safe/outdoor/sun_safety.html

[6]"Ticks: Geographic Distribution," Centers for Disease Control, http://www.cdc.gov/ticks/ geographic_distribution.html

[7]"Find a Doctor or Hospital Abroad," U.S. Department of State, http://travel.state.gov/travel/ tips/emergencies/emergencies_1195.html

Mara Gorman

Mara Gorman is an award-winning freelance writer and family travel blogger at The Mother of all Trips (motherofalltrips.com). The blog's name was inspired by a 13-month adventure across six states, three countries, and two continents that she took with her husband and toddler. Since that first extended trip, Mara has logged thousands of miles of travel with her children across North America and Europe.

Mara's lifestyle and travel articles have appeared in a variety of *USA Today* special-interest publications and on websites like AOL Travel. She is an avid skier, loves museums, and cultural travel, and has never met an ice cream that she didn't like. She also believes in serving global causes, especially those that help women and children; this belief is exemplified by her role as a board member of the travel blogging fundraiser Passports with Purpose.

Mara lives in Delaware with her husband and two school-age sons.

Mara Gorman

Mara Gorman

Lightning Source UK Ltd.
Milton Keynes UK
UKIC01n2100260914
239277UK00001B/3